MW00604081

Building on Ethereum

with Solidity and React

imajn

Published by Imajn, an imprint of Futurescale, Inc

ISBN: 978-1-7345521-0-2

For Kiska and Infinity.
We miss you, girls.

Preface

In this book, I discuss the various aspects of a project encompassing a non-trivial set of Ethereum smart contracts and the React application that communicates with them. It documents the eight month journey I spent building, deploying, and testing the system.

Along the way there were decisions to be researched and setbacks to overcome. This taught me a lot about the constraints, vulnerabilities, and strengths of the Ethereum blockchain. I'll impart much of that here, preparing you for developing a decentralized application (or "dApp") of your own.

I'll assume you're a web developer who has looked into Ethereum enough to know you want to try working on a small project with it. I won't attempt to make this book a canonical reference to Ethereum development. The field moves far too swiftly for that. Rather, I want to lead you through the decision points you'll encounter when you set up a project and grow it beyond trivial scope.

We will explore a project built with React and Solidity, but those aren't the only options by a long shot. The Ethereum Foundation and a vibrant community have made sure of that. Consequently, I did a lot of research, and to get through the analysis paralysis, I had to make a lot of hard choices. In this book, I'll give you the lay of the land that I wish I'd had going in.

Conventions Used in This Book

When filenames, folders, or contract names are referred to in body text, they will be italicized like this: *package.json, contracts/*, or *AccessControl*.

When language keywords, variable names, and function names are referred to in body text, they will appear in monospace like this: `uint256` or `msg.sender`, as will code blocks and terminal screen output.

You will have noticed above that hyphenation may occasionally break an inline code span or italicized word. In these cases, the hyphen is never part of the variable, keyword, filename, etc.

While live links are supported by eBook and PDF formats, print remains stubbornly unclickable. And if they are long, it's a pain to type them in. Therefore, web destinations used to support specific terms will be shortened using the Bitly URL-shortening service, unless they are already reasonably short. Rather than placing them in body text, they will be listed in a "Links" list at the end of the section where they are first mentioned, like this:

Links

Contact the Author
`cliffordhall.com/interrupt-me`

Table of Contents

CHAPTER ONE

The Project

In-App purchases represent an undeniably huge potential revenue stream for any game or application. Consider that Fortnite sold over 1 billion dollars worth of in-game purchases within a year of its inception. Most traditional game platforms are "walled gardens" where all the assets that gamers purchase come straight from the company who wrote the game. That's good for the company; they're the only source of magic swords. But for the players, frankly, it sucks.

With Ethereum, those assets could live on the public blockchain and actually be *owned* by the users, who could sell or trade them like CryptoKitties or any other ERC-721 Non-fungible Token (NFT). When a player tires of a game after a year or two, she could sell all her assets to other players to recoup her investment.

An interesting potential for apps built on Ethereum is that they can incorporate existing smart contracts and tokens that already live on the blockchain. For instance, Loom Networks' CryptoZombies feed on CryptoKitties, which are NFTs created by another app entirely. Game developers could choose to allow assets from other games to be used in their own, simply by choosing to support those NFTs, the way CryptoKitties can be used in various games in the "Kittyverse."

To be successful, you still need to write a great game or application, that much is certain. And while those that serve their users in this way may not extract the maximum revenue from every signup, they will almost certainly be rewarded by a grateful and loyal user base. I firmly believe that at some point in the near future, a major game that uses Ethereum for in-app purchases will be a tipping point. It will show users that they don't have to settle for games that provide an endless sinkhole to throw their money into, never to be seen again. After that, it will be a difficult proposition for old-school game shops to continue with their same economic model.

The project explored by this book, called In-App Pro Shop, aims to help Ethereum developers easily support in-app purchases as NFTs. It is open source and freely available on Github. Rather than leverage the project as a revenue stream for my company, I decided to open source and write about it instead. Not only will that have a greater chance of pushing adoption of Ethereum for in-app purchases, it's a great starting point for developers to learn Ethereum.

If you actually need this functionality, hopefully I've saved you some work. Feel free to get in touch if you have any questions about it. Even if you have no interest whatsoever in gaming or in-app purchases, this book should still give you a good introduction to the Ethereum development landscape. Plus, there is much to learn by investigating the mechanics of a non-trivial example.

Links

ERC-721 Standard
erc721.org

CryptoZombies
bit.ly/2XiLEfL

CryptoKitties
bit.ly/2FQNWwO

In-App Pro Shop
bit.ly/2KXnohH

Non-fungible Tokens (NFTs)
bit.ly/2J7SW2a

Fortnite has earned over $1 billion from in-game purchases
bit.ly/2YvnS1J

User Interface

There is a vast array of options available to us for building the system and and soon enough, we'll get into choosing the elements of what seems to be a reasonable setup for our tech stack, dependencies, and project structure.

But first, what are the moving parts of this system? How would someone use it to support in-app purchases to their game or application? These are the questions I want to clear up in this chapter.

The easiest way to start is by describing the user interface for the maintenance application that Shop Owners will use to create their Shops, populate them with Items to sell, and transfer balances out of the smart contract and into their Ethereum account.

By reviewing the scope of the dApp's features now, you'll have some context when we start researching what will be necessary to support it. And it will lend clarity to the rest of the book, as we deep dive into the contracts and their data structures as well as the client-side code.

The user interface that communicates with the blockchain to perform shop maintenance will need (at a minimum) the following features:

- Select the Shop Owner's Ethereum address
- Create Shops tied to the Shop Owner's address

- Select an existing Shop to maintain
- Display the Categories and Items in a selected Shop
- Add Categories to the Shop Owner's Shops
- Add Items to the Categories of the Shop Owner's Shops
- Report and withdraw the balances of the Shop Owner's Shops

Other functionality, such as selling items will be supported by our Ethereum smart contracts, but will be initiated from the Shop Owner's game or other application.

Also, a brief note on the design aesthetic. A gradient from deep blue to bright cyan is used to draw the eye to areas of interaction. The gradient is shown horizontally on the menu bar and on the shop display panels, where interactions happen on the right side. The gradient is shown vertically on forms where the key interaction (submit) appears at the bottom of the form. For accessibility, the color palette for menus, buttons, and form text was chosen for maximum contrast and readability.

Splash Screen

The user will need to have MetaMask installed, and the app will ask to connect with it at startup. Until that happens, we'll show the basic splash screen with a spinner.

Once the user has approved the connection to MetaMask and the app has received a list of the user's accounts, we can display menus and the form for creating a new Shop.

Accounts Menu

Unlike most web applications, we won't be asking for an email and password. Rather, we just need an Ethereum address. The *web3.js* library will take care of getting us the list of the user's available addresses, either from MetaMask or the local blockchain we'll run in development. One or more addresses will be available at startup, and we'll select the first one. If there are multiple addresses available, the user will be able to switch between them. Also, they can view the selected account on `etherscan.io`, if connected to a public network.

Create Shop Form

A Shop will have associated with it a name and description, as well as a fiat currency for setting prices. Prices need to be set in a stable fiat currency like USD, so the Shop Owner doesn't have to change them every time the value of Ether skyrockets or nosedives. If the price were set in Ether, then market fluctuations could suddenly make the item prohibitively expensive or dirt cheap. That makes it difficult to forecast revenue. If you expect a Magic Sword to cost 5 bucks, that's what it will cost.

Shops Menu

Shop Owners will be able to create any number of shops, and so, for the current Shop Owner's address, we need to provide a way to choose from their existing shops (if any).

The Shops menu will provide this list, a count of the items in the list (visible when the menu is open or closed), and a link to the Create Shop form, if we're not currently on the Splash Screen.

Shop Display

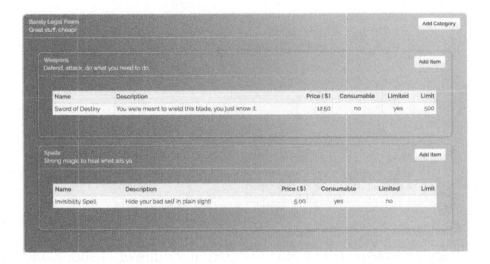

When the Shop Owner has created or selected a Shop, we'll display a panel with the Shop name and description in the header area. There will be a button for adding Categories to the Shop at the top right.

If there are any Categories, they will be displayed in their own sub-panels, with the Category name and description in the header area, along with a button for adding an Item to the Category.

Voucher System...

Add Category Form

A Category will just need a name and description. As with other forms on the site, we'll do some validation, in this case that the name is at least three characters long and the description is at least five. In the smart contracts, Categories are called SKU Types, and Items are called SKUs (Stock Keeping Units). SKU is a traditional term brick-and-mortar operations use to describe an item for sale. The terms Item and Category being more user friendly, are used on the UI.

Add Item Form

Items also require a name and description, and will have the same field validation as the Shop and Category forms. Additionally, we'll have a price, which represents an amount in the fiat currency of the shop, a floating point value with two decimal places. This field will prove interesting when we go to store or display it, because Solidity only supports integer values.

Also, we'll use a special component for price that allows the user to just enter the value without having to key in the decimal point. There are also a couple of checkboxes to indicate whether the Item is limited, or if it is consumable, e.g., a "magic potion" that can only be used once. If the item is limited, an extra field will be displayed to enter the maximum number of Items of this type that can be minted.

Maintenace app?

Shop Balance Menu

When a customer purchases an Item from a Shop (which will happen in the Shop Owner's application, not in this maintenance app), the Ethereum smart contract will take a fraction of the sale price as a "franchise fee" and the net will be added to the Shop balance.

When a Shop Owner selects their Shop in the maintenance app, the Balance menu will be shown. It will display the current balance for the Shop (in its defined fiat currency), and if non-zero, the Withdraw Shop Balance menu item will be enabled. Choosing that menu item will initiate the transaction, opening a MetaMask window to approve it. After the transaction has taken place the displayed available balance will be zero.

Summary

We have much work ahead of us, creating and testing the contracts and this user interface I've just described. But at least now it should be clear what the scope of the frontend work will be. Simple maintenance of the Shop, and the ability to withdraw any accrued balance from sales. Knowing what the UI will allow to the user to create sheds light on the requirements of the smart contracts that will support it.

CHAPTER TWO

Decisions, Decisions

Starting a new project, particularly one that doesn't quite match your previous experiences, is always exciting, but it can be a bit daunting.

A few questions that took me a while to answer were:

- What language(s) should I use?
- What blockchain tech stack do I need to get started?
- What framework(s) will I use to build the UI?
- What should the project structure look like?

In this chapter, I'll break these questions down and arrive at a place where we can move forward and start solving actual problems. The following sections discuss the above questions in detail, presenting the best options available at the time of this writing.

Language Choices

For the UI, we're going to go ahead and take browser-executed JavaScript as a given. It may seem arbitrary, but that describes almost everything in life, doesn't it?

It's not really that arbitrary, though.

Our application isn't going to be mobile because the use cases don't lend themselves to that. It's a maintenance application for creating an online store and populating it with digital goods for sale. While it could be done on a phone or tablet, realistically this is a desktop use case. And while it could be a standalone application, there's no need to get into that. Who wants to install an another application on their desktop for a use case that's as easily executed in a browser?

If you're developing for the browser, there are multiple options but they boil down to JavaScript and languages that compile to JavaScript. And while I love strong typing, classes, and interfaces, a lot of web developers don't.

Simply put, when building a single-page web application, it's hard to go wrong with pure JavaScript.

The truly tough decision comes in choosing an Ethereum language. If you're going to write smart contracts for Ethereum blockchain, you need a language that compiles down to something executable by the Ethereum Virtual Machine (EVM).

different ETH languages

When I began my project in early 2018, the options were roughly: Bamboo, LLL, Mutan, Serpent, Solidity, and Vyper.

At that time, Solidity was the most… *solid* solution. The other options were either seemingly on their way out, not fully usable yet, or not as well documented and supported by the community as Solidity.

I'm certain there'll be more options available to readers of this book in the future, so don't take it as a given that Solidity should be your only choice. These other projects have a lot of effort behind them and look to solve some of the issues Solidity has.

Here is a brief overview of the options I weighed in choosing the Ethereum contract language for this project.

Bamboo

This language is maintained by the Cornell University Blockchain Club. From its repository wiki:

Bamboo is a programming language for Ethereum contracts. Bamboo makes state transition explicit and avoids reentrance problems by default.

Smart contracts should reduce surprises. The code should reveal what can happen in which order, and the same ordering must be enforced mechanically. This is not done in the usual way of writing smart contracts where a smart contract is described as several interface functions.

...[T]he names of functions suggest the timing of the calls, but this ordering can only be enforced by careful timestamp checking or global state tracking in the body of the functions.

This language is designed to facilitate a particular style. So the language will not support features like:

- *loop constructs (for, while, ...). Due to the constant block gas limit, loops should be avoided and each iteration should be done in separate transactions.*
- *assignments into storage variables, except array elements. Instead of assigning a new value to a storage variable, the new value can be given as an argument in the continuation, e.g. return () then auction(new_highest_bidder, ...)*

Links

Bamboo
`bit.ly/2JrgL3Z`

LLL

LLL is one of the original Ethereum smart contract programming languages and provides a different perspective and programming discipline when compared to the ubiquitous Solidity language. According to the Ethereum Homestead Documentation:

Lisp Like Language (LLL) is a low level language similar to Assembly. It is meant to be very simple and minimalistic; essentially just a tiny wrapper over coding in EVM directly.

In particular, LLL doesn't hide from you the highly resource-constrained nature of the EVM and enables efficient use of those limited resources. LLL facilitates the creation of very clean EVM code whilst removing the worst of the pain of coding for the EVM directly: namely stack management and jump management.

Links

LLL in Ethereum Homestead Documentation
bit.ly/2XJfJtm

Introductory Series on LLL
bit.ly/30a8NTo

Mutan

Created and maintained by video game developer Jeffrey Wilcke (obscuren on GitHub), Mutan is written in the Go language. It was a precursor to Solidity and is now deprecated. From the code repository's README:

Mutan is a C-Like language for the Ethereum project. Mutan supports a full, dynamic higher level language that compiles to native Ethereum Assembler.

Links

Mutan Repository
`bit.ly/2FSdidH`

Apparent Deprecation Notice
`bit.ly/32aLRVQ`

Serpent

Written in C++, Serpent appears to be an advanced choice. Vitalik Buterin, creator of Ethereum considers it out-of-date tech, since it doesn't have enough safety precautions. From its repository README:

Serpent is an assembly language that compiles to EVM code that is extended with various high-level features. It can be useful for writing code that requires low-level opcode manipulation as well as access to high-level primitives like the ABI.

Being a low-level language, Serpent is NOT RECOMMENDED for building applications unless you really really know what you're doing. The creator recommends Solidity as a default choice, LLL if you want close-to-the-metal optimizations, or Vyper if you like its features though it is still experimental.

Links

Serpent Repository
bit.ly/2KWgE3y

PSA
bit.ly/2xpsjPF

Solidity

This is the Ethereum Project's default language. From its documentation website:

Solidity is an object-oriented, high-level language for implementing smart contracts. Smart contracts are programs which govern the behavior of accounts within the Ethereum state.

Solidity was influenced by C++, Python and JavaScript and is designed to target the Ethereum Virtual Machine (EVM).

Solidity is statically typed, supports inheritance, libraries and complex user-defined types among other features.

With Solidity you can create contracts for uses such as voting, crowdfunding, blind auctions, and multi-signature wallets.

Links

Solidity Docs
`bit.ly/2XkrtTw`

Vyper

This is another language maintained by the Ethereum Project and written in Python. From the repository README:

Vyper is a smart contract development language built with the following goals:

- *Security - it should be possible and natural to build secure smart contracts in Vyper.*
- *Language and compiler simplicity - the language and the compiler implementation should strive to be simple.*
- *Auditability - Vyper code should be maximally human-readable. Furthermore, it should be maximally difficult to write misleading code. Simplicity for the reader is more important than simplicity for the writer, and simplicity for readers with low prior experience with Vyper (and low prior experience with programming in general) is particularly important.*

Some examples of what Vyper does NOT have and why:

- *Modifiers - e.g. in Solidity you can do function foo() mod1 { ... }, where mod1 can be defined elsewhere in the code to include a check that is done before execution, a check that is done after execution, some state changes, or possibly other things. Vyper does not have this, because it makes it too easy to write misleading code. mod1 just looks too innocuous for something that could add* arbitrary pre-conditions, post-conditions or state changes. Also, it encourages people to write code where the execution jumps around the file, harming auditability. The usual use case for a modifier is something that performs a single check before execution of a program; our recommendation is to simply inline these checks as asserts.

- *Class inheritance - requires people to jump between multiple files to understand what a program is doing, and requires people to understand the rules of precedence in case of conflicts (which class' function X is the one that's actually used?). Hence, it makes code too complicated to understand.*

- *Inline assembly - adding inline assembly would make it no longer possible to Ctrl+F for a variable name to find all instances where that variable is read or modified.*

- *Function overloading - This can cause lots of confusion on which function is called at any given time. Thus it's easier to write misleading code (foo("hello") logs "hello" but foo("hello", "world") steals your funds). Another problem with function overloading is that it makes the code much harder to search through as you have to keep track on which call refers to which function.*

- *Operator overloading - waaay too easy to write misleading code (what do you mean "+" means "send all my money to the developer"? I didn't catch the part of the code that says that!).*

- *Recursive calling - cannot set an upper bound on gas limits, opening the door for gas limit attacks.*

- *Infinite-length loops - cannot set an upper bound on gas limits, opening the door for gas limit attacks.*

- *Binary fixed point - decimal fixed point is better, because any decimal fixed point value written as a literal in code has an exact representation, whereas with binary fixed point approximations are often required (e.g. 0.2 -> 0.001100110011..., which needs to be truncated), leading to unintuitive results, e.g. in python 0.3 + 0.3 + 0.3 + 0.1 != 1.*

Vyper does NOT strive to be a 100% replacement for everything that can be done in Solidity; it will deliberately forbid things or make things harder if it deems fit to do so for the goal of increasing security.

Links

Vyper Repo
bit.ly/2NvSCP0

Blockchain Stack Choices

This set of choices is a bit more nuanced.

I'd already made the decision to work with Ethereum, because its smart contracts and Non-fungible Tokens like CryptoKitties were what had motivated me to build this thing in the first place. That choice was axiomatic.

All I knew at the outset was that the project would encompass one or more Ethereum smart contracts representing a virtual store, and a so-called "dApp" — a web application that allowed the user (a game or application creator) to maintain that store. Then purchasing and minting of items as NFTs would be supported by the contract but it would be up to the developer to implement the user interface for that since it would be part of their game or application.

For our part, it follows that we will need to authenticate shop owners and authorize them to take certain actions within the shop maintenance application. Further, we need to commit transactions to the blockchain on their behalf and respond to events coming from the blockchain. Our smart contracts must also adhere to identified best practices; they will handle currency, so avoiding the traps others have fallen into is paramount.

Authenticating and Authorizing

As a web developer, I was used to implementing a password-based authentication scheme, perhaps optionally offering OAuth so that users could instead choose a trusted auth provider such as Facebook or Twitter.

But in this scenario, the only thing that matters is that the user be the verified owner of a blockchain address which can send and receive ETH, the currency of the Ethereum blockchain. They won't be interacting with other users, just setting up shops and transferring out the balances from sales. As such, user profiles and traditional authentication processes are completely unnecessary.

But how do we verify that the user owns a given address? We need an Ethereum-aware browser or wallet to act as an intermediary.

I chose to test with MetaMask, but there are a number of options, I'm certain more will have cropped by the time you read this. I've been following the MetaMask project on GitHub, and it has been well maintained.

Remember that your users may expect your application to interact with plugins or browsers other than MetaMask. The decision here is merely what to test with starting out. You should weigh some of the options and understand the unique tradeoffs they may represent.

What follows is a brief survey of the landscape at the moment. It is by no means complete; there are new blockchain wallets launching every day it seems. Note that as a developer, this explosion of Web3 providers presents a hurdle. How do you decide which wallets to support with your dApp? How much effort will be required to integrate each one?

Check

Coinbase Wallet

Coinbase Wallet is owned by a popular crypto exchange. It is a mobile crypto wallet that allows interaction with dApps. It also works other coins like Bitcoin, not just Ethereum. However, it's mobile only, so testing your app from a desktop browser with it is out of the question.

Links

Coinbase Wallet Website
`bit.ly/2Xk5SWF`

Dapper

Dapper is made by Dapper Labs, the company that created CryptoKitties. It is a smart contract-based wallet, so Dapper claims, even the owners can't touch your stuff. Currently it is only available for Chrome, with iOS and Android support promised. A differentiator is that it offers free gas on certain dApps that they have partnered with.

From the Dapper website:

What Dapper can do for you

- **Never lose your stuff** - *If you lose your device or password, Dapper offers account recovery without having access or control over your stuff.*
- **Freedom from fees** - *Dapper teams up with the best blockchain games and experiences to give you free transactions, so you can focus on having fun.*
- **One-click convenience** - *With Dapper, you can buy cryptocurrency and collectibles with a credit card, and know all your digital treasures are safe.*

Links

Dapper Website
`meetdapper.com`

2 step auth...

Fortmatic

An interesting but more involved option, Fortmatic requires our app to integrate with their SDK in order to access the user's account. When a user goes to make a transaction, they are sent a text with a code on their mobile phone, which they must then enter into the application to proceed.

It does appear to be a very secure system. So if you are implementing a system where you are concerned not only about your dApp having access to the users' accounts, but also about their specific security practices, you may want to delve more deeply into Fortmatic's offering.

From their Developer FAQ:

We've adopted the cryptographic anchor security architecture. Users' encrypted private keys are managed and safeguarded by the Hardware Security Modules (HSMs) in our system.

In a canonical data exfiltration attack in organizations without cryptographic anchor architecture, hackers can enter a system and download users' encrypted private keys, and then crack them freely offline, with their own infrastructure. The organizations won't even know that they are exploited before realizing the funds are stolen.

With Fortmatic's cryptographic anchor architecture, hackers will have to attempt to crack the encrypted private keys within Fortmatic's infrastructure, which means hackers' progress can be detected, impeded and monitored. And with this adversarial environment, the damage of a compromise can be significantly mitigated.

Links

Fortmatic Website
`fortmatic.com`

Fortmatic Developer FAQ
`bit.ly/2ugf6do`

MetaMask

The MetaMask browser plugin runs on the Chrome, Firefox, Opera, and Brave browsers. It acts as an intermediary between our application and the user's Ethereum address(es). This is important if you want to test your application from the desktop.

Users install MetaMask, configure it with one or more existing Ethereum addresses (or create some), and secure them with a password. After that, whenever they load our application, it asks for confirmation that they want to connect the app to their currently selected account.

From a developer perspective, you have to request that Meta-Mask export the user's accounts. It will not automatically export them anymore. Due to another blockchain stack decision described shortly, we won't actually have to do that ourselves.

From a security perspective, the user should export and save their "Seed Words" (also called a mnemonic) in a secure location, as that's the only way to access their accounts should they encounter a catastrophic loss or system crash. They can import a mnemonic to access an existing account.

From their website:

MetaMask is a bridge that allows you to visit the distributed web of tomorrow in your browser today. It allows you to run Ethereum dApps right in your browser without running a full Ethereum node.

MetaMask includes a secure identity vault, providing a user interface to manage your identities on different sites and sign blockchain transactions.

Links

MetaMask Website
metamask.io

Trust Wallet

This mobile wallet / browser solution allows the user to access dApps natively. Of course, since it's mobile only, testing your from the desktop isn't possible using Trust Wallet.

From the Trust Wallet website:

- *Fully functioning Web3 browser that can be used to interact with any decentralized application (dApp)*
- *Meticulously crafted tool that provides a seamless, simple and secure connection between you, Ethereum network, and any dApp*
- *Integrated interface that is fully optimized for mobile so you can enjoy the content designed specifically for your device*

Links

Trust Wallet Website
trustwallet.com

uPort

Unlike most of their singularly focused competition, uPort is building quite a few things. Consequently, if you go to their website, you may find yourself lost in a thicket of conjecture about the future of the blockchain and how they are working hard on many fronts to make it happen. If you're interested in their wallet, however, I suggest going to the Apple Store or Google Play to find out more and download.

From the uPort app description on the App Store:

uPort mobile is a secure mobile self-sovereign identity wallet for that gives you complete control over your identity and personal data.

With uPort mobile app you can:

- Create an identity on the Ethereum blockchain network
- Securely log-in to applications without passwords
- Manage your personal information and verifications
- Approve Ethereum transactions and digitally sign files

This mobile wallet is your connection to the uPort platform, an interoperable identity network for a secure, private, decentralized web. uPort provides open protocols for decentralized identity and interoperable messaging that enable trusted source attribution for all web communication. By allowing message recipients to trust message senders without centralized servers, we can create an entirely new framework for building applications, and many developers are already building on this system.

Links

uPort Website
uport.me

uPort on Apple Store
apple.co/2OsW7UC

uPort on Google Play
bit.ly/35McgdV

Interacting with the Blockchain

From the browser side of things, the lowest-level library you'll need to familiarize yourself with is *web3.js*. It is the official Java-Script Ethereum API.

Now, if you're a .NET developer, you might choose to add the Nethereum library, which essentially wraps *web3.js* and provides a better integration with your .NET code. We won't be going down that road in this book, however, we'll just be using JavaScript and *web3.js*.

MetaMask (which we'll be testing with) provides an instance of *web3.js* that your app can use once it's initialized, so you're able to implement transfers and other actions on behalf of the user. And while we could use *web3.js* alone to communicate with the blockchain, I chose to add Drizzle into the mix as well. Drizzle is part of the Truffle Framework, and among other things, it automatically connects your app to MetaMask and gets its *web3.js* instance, along with the selected account.

We also need to test, deploy, and debug the contracts, not just talk to them from within our application. For security and speed of testing, we want to run a local blockchain so that we're not having to put all this stuff out there on a public network as we develop.

Setting up that local node is itself a decision; there are a lot of Ethereum clients to pick from.

Repo of Code in OUR Computer

I chose Ganache-CLI for this project, mainly because of its broad community support, but that doesn't mean it's the best option. I will say it has been very reliable for me during development and testing. Since I'm not concerned with setting up a mining operation connected to a public network, I'm still happy with my decision. But as always, you should evaluate the options yourself.

We also need a command line interface to talk to that local blockchain. For that, there is Truffle — the centerpiece of The Truffle Framework, of which Drizzle and Ganache are also parts. Truffle allows us to compile our Solidity contracts, deploy them, execute tests, debug transactions, and more. It's well-documented and maintained.

While this list is by no means complete, for the rest of this section, we'll discuss a few prominent Ethereum clients that seem to be fully (or nearly) operational options at this time: Aleth (formerly cpp-ethereum), EthereumJ/Harmony, EthereumJS-vm, Geth, Ganache (formerly TestRPC), Nethermind, Parity, and Trinity.

Aleth

Aleth (previously cpp-ethereum) is written in C++, and is a fully working Ethereum client. However, the documentation does warn:

This project is not suitable for Ethereum mining because the support for GPU mining has been dropped some time ago including the ethminer tool.

Links

Aleth Repository
`bit.ly/2XmbXBJ`

EthereumJ / Harmony

Part of the official Ethereum Project, EthereumJ is a pure-Java implementation of the Ethereum protocol. There is no support for JSON-RPC, however so this is not a great option if you're talking to it from a web client. For that there is Harmony, which is built on EthereumJ. Both projects were recently deprecated and are only included here for those with interest in the mechanics of a Java-based Ethereum client.

Links

EthereumJ Repo
bit.ly/2XluuhB

Harmony Repo
bit.ly/2RQDOJf

Ethereumjs-vm

This project implements the Ethereum Virtual Machine (EVM) in JavaScript, and is part of the larger EthereumJS project. Though it might be possible to use this implementation on its own, etheremjs-vm seems to be a low-level implementation that other projects out there build upon. From their documentation:

Main focus of EthereumJS is to provide high-quality and robust implementations of core Ethereum infrastructure technologies (virtual machine), protocols (devp2p) and data structures (merkle tree).

Other related projects you might want to check out as well are e.g.:

*   *web3.js (Ethereum JavaScript API)*
*   *ethers.js (Ethereum Wallet implementation and library)*
*   *Truffle (Development Framework)*
*   *embark (dApp Framework)*
*   *Remix*

Most of the projects above also make use of some of our base-layer libraries. EthereumJS libraries are also used by various other actors within the ecosystem like MetaMask, 0x or Augur.

One strong emphasis of EthereumJS work is on maintaining and further developing a robust and up-to-date JavaScript virtual machine implementation (ethereumjs-vm).

Main tasks around this are:

*   *Updating the VM on new hardforks*

- *Targeting compliance with the latest consensus test suite releases*
- *Implementing feature requests from the community (Truffle, Remix, others), e.g. to provide better debugging functionalities*
- *Ongoing refactoring work to open up new use cases*

Links

EthereumJS Repositories
`bit.ly/2JsxR1w`

Ganache

There are two versions of Ganache (formerly TestRPC). Ganache-CLI , the command line version, is lightweight and friendly, perfect for starting out. Ganache is a GUI-based version. Cute, but not useful for day-to-day dev work.

Both implementations are part of the Truffle Framework, which also includes Truffle (a console for communicating with Ganache) and Drizzle, a JavaScript client library for communicating with the blockchain from your application. This suite of tools is one of the most well-supported and well documented options out there, and what we'll be building with in this book.

Links

Ganache-CLI Repo
bit.ly/30dgdFD

Ganache Repo
bit.ly/2YxfoH6

Truffle Framework Website
bit.ly/2Yzuz2E

Geth

Geth (go-ethereum) is an Ethereum node built in the Go language. This is a full implementation that can be connected to the main net and used for mining operations, transferring funds, sending transactions, exploring block history, and more. It is useful when it's time to connect to public testnets.

Links

Geth Repository
`bit.ly/2Lzns6B`

Nethermind

The .NET Core Ethereum Client for Linux, Windows, and MacOS. If you're into .NET development, this is an option you may want to look into. *If not, then never mind.*

Links

Nethermind Website
`bit.ly/2XQ878a`

Nethermind Repo
`bit.ly/2Nwj5f9`

Parity

The Parity Ethereum client is built in the Rust language. From the Parity Website:

Built for mission-critical use - Miners, service providers, and exchanges need fast synchronisation and maximum uptime. Parity Ethereum provides the core infrastructure essential for speedy and reliable services.

- *Clean, modular codebase for easy customisation*
- *Advanced CLI-based client*
- *Minimal memory and storage footprint*
- *Synchronise in hours, not days with Warp Sync*
- *Modular for light integration into your service or product*

Links

Parity Website
`bit.ly/2XjzmDP`

Trinity

The Trinity Ethereum client is based on a Python implementation of the Ethereum Virtual Machine called PY-EVM, which contains the low-level primitives for the existing Ethereum 1.0 chain as well as emerging support for the upcoming Ethereum 2.0 / Serenity spec.

At the time of this writing, the Trinity client is in an alpha release stage and is not suitable for mission critical production use cases.

Links

Trinity Website
bit.ly/2NwtZS4

Py-evm Repository
bit.ly/2YuWsJd

Implementing Best Practices

When we enter an unfamiliar realm of software development, sorting out our options can seem overwhelming. We can find ourselves making decisions arbitrarily, due to the sheer volume. Sometimes those decisions lead us to basins of stability; set-ups where we can apply ourselves to our tasks daily and make measurable progress. If not, we revisit this decisions until we find a stack that works for us.

Not only do we want to assemble a stack that works, but we want to be sure that what we build with it makes sense to others who use that same stack. We owe it to future developers who'll join our team or inherit our code. And to users who'll have to contend with the errors and omissions we've made along the way. So, once we have a stable set of development tools, it's important that we seek out the best practices the community has identified for using them.

This section only addresses Solidity, the Ethereum language discussed in this book and used in the associated project. We've reached the level of detail where it no longer makes sense to lay out every option for all alternative stack combinations. But this should still give you a pointer in the direction of where to look next if you're planning to work with a different set of tools.

Linters

Just like the linters we use with JavaScript which tell us when we are making stylistic and syntactic booboos in our code, for Solidity there are several.

Solhint

Install with **npm** and configure with a simple JSON file. It's lovely and keeps all your code nice and tidy, so that other Solidity developers will feel right at home with it. If you use the IntelliJ WebStorm IDE, you can install it as a plugin. Because of this integration, I've used Solhint in my workflow. Sublime text editor also offers a Solhint plugin.

Links

Solhint
bit.ly/2S1kPMl

Webstorm Solhint
bit.ly/2YBfNso

Sublime Solhint
bit.ly/30b8zvu

Ethlint (formerly solium)

Install with **npm** and configure with a simple JSON file. You invoke it from the command line. The project website makes it apparent that Ethlint has aspirations beyond your normal linter.

Links

Ethlint
`ethlint.com`

Linter-solidity

An Atom editor plugin, so you install it with **apm** and live Solidity linting support is then integrated into your editor.

Links

Linter-solidity
`bit.ly/3251s9L`

Vulnerabilities

Since Solidity smart contracts interact with and hold actual currency, it's important that we stay abreast of the known vulnerabilities. There are a number of known attacks out there, some of which have drained prominent apps of hundreds of millions of dollars worth of Ether.

To guard against some of these hacks, for instance, we need to make certain that overflows and underflows don't happen when we do math operations since we're using unsigned integers. And we need to be sure that we don't transfer funds to another contract or address before adjusting our internal accounting. That can trigger a 'reentrancy' attack where we transfer out funds and the receiving contract calls us again before we've recorded the details of the transfer, withdrawing again. The evil loop continues until there's no funds left. This is just a taste of what lies in wait for the unwary Solidity developer.

There are a number of good resources to help you get up to speed on the threats. Consensys has a list of known hacks on their best practices site. An in-depth article on Hackernoon called "Hackpedia" by Vaibhav Saini should be considered required reading. Securify, an organization funded by an Ethereum Foundation grant, has a security scanner for smart contracts. Open Zeppelin has a wargame called Ethernaut, where each level is a smart contract that needs to be hacked to move forward. You can even add your own levels to the game at their repository.

Links

Open Zeppelin
`bit.ly/2J7tIAV`

Ethernaut
`bit.ly/327on49`

Securify Contract Scanner
`bit.ly/324e0hn`

Consensys Ethereum Smart Contract Best Practices
`bit.ly/2FSej5v`

Hackpedia: 16 Solidity Hacks/Vulnerabilities, their Fixes and Real World Examples
`bit.ly/2NuLyCf`

Interoperability

Further, we have to properly implement the standards we work with, such as the ERC-721 NFTs that this application will mint. There are published interfaces that define the functions, arguments, and return values. We can implement them from scratch (and possibly make dangerous mistakes), or we can stand on the backs of giants and use peer-reviewed public libraries like Open Zeppelin's, which I've chosen to include in my own project. I often eschew dependencies in my Javascript code, choosing to write some essential bits on my own. However in the case of Solidity, particularly being new to it, I decided to focus on writing only those parts of my app that were unique. Let seasoned pros and the 'many eyes' principle of open source handle the underlying grunt work where possible.

Links

ERC-721 Standard
erc721.org

The Ultimate List of ERC Standards You Need To Know
bit.ly/307m9jm

User Interface Choices

Since we're building both a set of smart contracts and a user interface to interact with them, we have a few more technology stack decisions to consider.

- Which application framework will I use?
- Which component library will I use?
- How will I style my components?

These questions will be a little more familiar to the average web developer, and you'll probably have your own leanings on each. Fortunately, they don't matter *that much* in the big scheme of things. Practically any UI stack will do. None is objectively any better than the next with regard to communicating with the blockchain. So I'll mostly just be describing the choices I made in the In App Pro Shop front end.

Application Framework

The application framework we choose makes very little difference in the long run. Use whatever kit you're feeling at the moment to get those buttons up on the screen and move the data from point A to point B. Personally, I'm handy with React for layout and Redux for state management at the moment, so that's the stack I picked. You could as easily use Angular, Vue, or even jQuery if you were so inclined.

Now, if you're going to use React, there are TruffleBoxes to give you a shrink-wrapped answer to this decision. It's worthwhile to look at them for an idea about what a fully formed project could look like. For all you Angular folks, there's a a TruffleBox as well as a standalone boilerplate project for you on GitHub. And of course, there's a TruffleBox for Vue, if that's your preference. There are a million other application frameworks and many of them probably have boilerplate projects for working with Truffle framework. I'll let Google help you with that.

I found myself throwing out more stuff from the React TruffleBox than I was keeping, and so I ended up taking it all under advisement and starting from scratch.

Links

TruffleBoxes
`bit.ly/327dTBD`

Angular Truffle Boilerplate
`bit.ly/322ONUJ`

Component Library

You could just use standard HTML buttons and inputs and style them from scratch, but that's a little tedious if you don't have a dedicated UX person on your team. If you're like me, you'd rather get up and running with a serviceable set of components without having to spend too much effort.

A couple of good options are Bootstrap and Material Design. If you use Angular, Vue, or React, you can get implementations of both these kits that will work with your application framework.

I chose React-Bootstrap this time around. Not because of any advantage over Material Design or other options out there, it's just simple, and this is a fairly simple app.

Links

React-Bootstrap
bit.ly/2FQXebY

React Material UI
material-ui.com

Styling Components

Even though I've chosen React-Bootstrap for the component library, I still need to come up with a theme for my app so it doesn't just look like the standard, out-of-box controls.

In React, there are a number of ways to do this.

- Standard CSS
- CSS Pre-compilers (LESS/SASS)
- CSS in JS

I went with CSS in JS, because I have long thought that the separation of HTML and CSS was a pointless separation of concerns that's more trouble than it's worth. As your CSS (or SCSS) files grow, they do so in an unsatisfying way that is often full of duplication. I like the CSS in JS approach of isolating styling within components.

To keep it clean, I also used Styled Components to create a custom component kit and theme for the app. While the components in that kit all use React-Bootstrap, they could be refactored to use pure HTML and CSS. This would remove the dependency altogether. The accumulation of technical debt associated with the React-Bootstrap decision is contained in that kit. If you're interested in the philosophy behind the front-end theme, I wrote an in depth article about this approach with code samples on the CSS-Tricks website.

Links

Styled Components
`bit.ly/2XMMZ2I`

Iterating a React Design with Styled Components
`bit.ly/30debVN`

Project Structure Choices

If you start with a boilerplate project then you can just move right along, but I wanted as much control over the structure as possible. So, like a mountain goat defying logic and gravity, I decided to go my own way. That's not to say I that I didn't inherit a bunch of structural requirements by choices I'd made earlier, I did.

First, I considered whether to make separate projects for the client and the blockchain stuff, since there is different tech involved with each. Would it end up being an ugly mess if I tried to mash it all together? In the end, I decided to go with a monorepo, just to keep from having to launch and switch back and forth between two IDE instances.

When I say I inherited more than one structural requirement based on previous choices, I mean:

- React (if you use react-scripts or create-react-app) imposes some specific structure – the *public* template folder, the absolute requirement that all source code be included in the *src* folder, and its production *output* folder is called build.
- Truffle's default configuration looks for a *contracts* folder, a *migrations* folder, a *test* folder, and creates a *build* folder for the compiled contracts, which obviously conflicts with the React output *build* folder.

- Also, I found my React code needed to load the compiled Solidity contracts, and since React needs any imported files to be under the *src* folder, I had to configure Truffle to output builds into *src/abi*.

Although all the requirements weren't present at the beginning of the project, ultimately, I ended up with top level folders for:

- Smart contract sources
- Project documentation
- Migration scripts which compile and deploy the contracts to the blockchain
- Scripts that create mock data on the blockchain for manually testing the app
- The React HTML template and assets
- React app sources
- Smart contract tests

And based upon the various tech stack decisions, the basic dependencies were: *React, Redux, React-Scripts, React-Bootstrap, Styled-Components, Epic-Spinners, Drizzle, OpenZeppelin, Web3, Babel, Ganache-CLI, Truffle Contract, Jest, Chai, Mocha,* and *Redux Mock-StoreRegenerator*

Links

In-App Pro Shop Repository
`bit.ly/2FQmKhL`

Summary

There are a lot of ways you can go about building, testing, and deploying Ethereum smart contracts and the applications that talk to them. After a survey of the various choices, we've settled on a tech stack that will let us move forward.

Our app will use:

- **Solidity** for writing contracts
- **MetaMask** for connecting our browser-based application with the blockchain
- **Ganache-CLI** for a local Ethereum client
- **Solhint** for checking Solidity syntax and style
- **Open Zeppelin** base contracts for SafeMath, Role-based Access Control, and ERC-721 implementation
- **React & Redux** in for frontend architecture
- **React-bootstrap & Styled-Components** for UI components
- A monorepo project structure containing both contracts and UI

Fortunately, I've already done the hard part of making all these parts work with each other. The project is available on Github. Now all you need to do is download it and set up your local environment to work with it. That's what we'll get into next.

CHAPTER THREE

Local Environment

So far, we've reviewed the user interface functionality required for interacting with our smart contracts, chosen a tech stack, and settled upon a project structure.

That said, this is not one of those tutorials where there are lots of intermediate states where not much is working. The project itself has been built and fully operates, we will just be exploring it in stepwise fashion throughout the book.

We can now turn our attention to the following:

- Setting up the toolchain to support local development.
- Testing the contracts to be certain that our local blockchain is in order.

- Configuring MetaMask to use a deterministically created local account.
- Building and launching the application in a browser.
- Connecting the app to the local account via MetaMask.

By the end of this chapter, you should have all the necessary tools installed and the project up and running on a local machine.

If you don't want to install the project and all the tools right now, you can just skip over the setup instructions below and follow along with the discussion, referring to the code on Github.

Project Setup

In this section, we're going to install and Node and NPM, get the project from Github, install its Node modules, and install Ganache-CLI and Truffle globally.

Install Node & NPM

As with most modern web development projects, you'll need Node and its package manager NPM installed, so if you don't have them, go install Node and NPM will come along with it.

At the time of this writing, Node 12 and Truffle 5 are not playing nicely together. See the link for more details. My current advice is to install Node version 10 or 11.

Links

Node & NPM
`bit.ly/2XL2nwD`

Node 12 + Truffle = No Go
`bit.ly/33aslbD`

Get the Project

Get the latest version of the In-App Pro Shop project from Github. You can download a zip file or use git to clone it by running the following command in the folder where you'd like to install the project:

```
git clone https://github.com/cliffhall/in-app-pro-shop.git
```

If you don't have a git client installed, it's never to late to join the fun. Either way, when you're done you should have an *in-app-pro-shop* folder with the project source in it.

Links

In-App Pro Shop Repository
```
bit.ly/2FQmKhL
```

Installing Git
```
bit.ly/2Xkon1Q
```

Install Node Modules

In a Terminal window (or on Windows, a Command Prompt), navigate to the project folder and install the Node modules.

```
cd path/to/in-app-pro-shop
npm install
```

What were all those modules we just installed?

They're configured in *package.json,* and we touched on them briefly at the end of Chapter 2. They resulted from the a tree of decisions we traversed about what to build on.

The main dependencies are:

- **React-scripts** for managing webpack configuration, compilation, testing, code watching, local server.
- **Babel-core** for ES6/7 support.
- **Redux-thunk** middleware for asynchronous action creators.
- **React-bootstrap** for UI components.
- **React-app-rewired** for webpack config overrides to support Styled Components.
- **Styled-components** for easy application of CSS in JS.
- **Drizzle** and **Drizzle-react** for interacting with the blockchain and keeping data fresh.

- **Openzeppelin-solidity** base contracts for ERC721 tokens, role-based access control, safe math, etc.

Links

React-scripts
bit.ly/2NuOlva

Babel-core
bit.ly/2Jq50us

Redux-thunk
bit.ly/2xsNTCL

React-bootstrap
bit.ly/2FQXebY

React-app-rewired
bit.ly/2NyYeYE

Styled-components
bit.ly/2JaHyTf

Drizzle
bit.ly/2XpUVYd

Drizzle-react
bit.ly/2KVulzF

Openzeppelin-solidity
bit.ly/2J7tIAV

Verify Environment

In this section, we will ensure that everything is installed and setup properly. First, we'll start up Ganache-CLI which will act as our local blockchain. Next, we'll start Truffle Console, which we can then use to deploy our smart contracts and run our unit tests against them.

Once we're certain our contracts can be communicated with, we'll move on to building and testing the React client.

We'll use some of the info that Ganache-CLI reports on startup to configure the MetaMask browser plugin with a few accounts so that the app can connect to our accounts and initiate blockchain transactions on our behalf.

Also, it would be nice to see that the app is working properly even before we attempt to add data to the contracts via its forms. In order to do that, we'll create some mock data for it to read, using Truffle Console to execute a few scripts.

Start Ganache

If you followed the instructions in the Setup section, you should be ready to startup the local blockchain. To do that, you'll run an npm script in *package.json* called `ganache:start`.

```
"ganache:start": "ganache-cli -p 7545 -d -m 'cabbage inflict
doctor valve address roast bring club fiber celery lab render' -l
8000000",
```

This script invokes *ganache-cli* passing arguments that define the port number (7545), a gas limit that roughly matches what the mainnet and testnets are running (8000000), that it should run in deterministic mode (meaning that it will generate the same default set of accounts every time), and the twelve-word mnemonic (which generates the random seed used for account generation, and is required in deterministic mode).

We need to run in deterministic mode so that the MetaMask plugin can use the same hard-coded account numbers each time we interact with our contracts.

Launch a new Terminal window and run the following command:

```
npm run ganache:start
```

You should see something like the following output:

```
> in-app-pro-shop@1.0.0 ganache:start /Users/cliff/Documents/in-
app-pro-shop
> ganache-cli -p 7545 -d -m 'cabbage inflict doctor valve address
roast bring club fiber celery lab render' -l 8000000

Ganache CLI v6.2.3 (ganache-core: 2.3.1)

Available Accounts
==================
(0) 0xea5f1f147332e32a0dbbf25f4cbcb78d8ba879ce (~100 ETH)
(1) 0x8b7bb2c31bc7e02d84060ca87e8218cb3b57678d (~100 ETH)
(2) 0xf406df13b7f818ac7d3aa1b5a0e6319e1504b854 (~100 ETH)
(3) 0xae9acc448924d863c7e26bfa4b03d13931fa379c (~100 ETH)
(4) 0x250f9ffc17fc1e7198987ced09f4c1657c9dd584 (~100 ETH)
(5) 0x80fb1ee91b8208779454fb4f2e9e6022eda8f376 (~100 ETH)
(6) 0x0ebb63c29d8fcd217c877b0f20286670da7ba8c6 (~100 ETH)
(7) 0x2a6ad377c91e3951b648b4e1693ccd718b849e5e (~100 ETH)
(8) 0x486756d0ef7bc7b645ff366de76e5db012a815d2 (~100 ETH)
(9) 0x14b3bd4a1311d7ad688e1adc506f0c25fef350f3 (~100 ETH)

Private Keys
==================
(0) 0x55d22a8b7857fd66f8e1a456c580c8f19575e0ed0caeed6e101c5-
da82610e21f
(1) 0xa57f9b9a94e8cfb14-
daacb294933b841a796353a27d309785f5067c9fc3197fd
(2) 0xce0da61305b7287bf01ec01662caad381a33ca33cd6268c277efe-
f0c161794cf
(3) 0x21a1e0a293424aefef82b9117bf5078a3d-
c3a5f0239117145422525840b1253e
(4) 0x89db56534d88790e58270a9c58f2bb7c0490d962f0a3f2255bbcb-
b3a7014d875
(5) 0x7c60fa1ecc701b1b909fce256511eae32d83faa56c18c5d62823b5-
fad88c6da8
(6) 0x86cf570418e-
f0188b4dea2e6f7729871142f15962a66de93637b079213c28ea0
(7) 0x5cae7fcd316b938a205e01037123b625fc71504667f4333c4f04f-
b2ae622af85
(8) 0xa4de0d798256087c15a1eb0a9a06539e8527e690ba419b17050871328-
ca80d86
(9) 0x16987137ae70739e6535b042c1ec2d51a885bab0e6b143180c6e45d-
fec15b96f

HD Wallet
```

```
==================
Mnemonic:       cabbage inflict doctor valve address roast bring
club fiber celery lab render
Base HD Path:  m/44'/60'/0'/0/{account_index}

Gas Price
==================
20000000000

Gas Limit
==================
8000000

Listening on 127.0.0.1:7545
```

Note that Ganache-CLI has initialized the balances of all ten default accounts with one hundred ETH each. Further, it has listed the private keys for each of the accounts it generated. Remember this because later, we'll need to configure the first three accounts with MetaMask in the browser using their private keys.

Start Truffle Console

The Truffle console lets you deploy your smart contracts, send and debug blockchain transactions, and more. It needs to know a few things about how to connect to the blockchain when it comes up. This is configured in the file called *truffle.js*.

```
const path = require('path');
const HDWalletProvider = require("truffle-hdwallet-provider");

// Replace with your MetaMask Seed Phrase
const mnemonic = 'cabbage inflict doctor . . .';

// Use your Infura project id
const url = 'https://ropsten.infura.io/v3/YOUR_PROJECT_ID_HERE';

module.exports = {
    contracts_build_directory: path.join(__dirname, "src/abi"),
    networks: {
        development: {
            host: "127.0.0.1",
            port: 7545,
            from: "0xea5f1f147332e32a0dbbf25f4cbcb78d8ba879ce",
            network_id: "*",
            gas: 8000000
        },
        ropsten: {
            provider: () => new HDWalletProvider(mnemonic, url,
1),
            network_id: "3"
        }
    }
};
```

This file defines where the compiled contracts will go and our local development network's parameters, namely the host, port, gas limit, and default source account for transactions.

In a new Terminal window, run the following command:

```
truffle console
```

And since it isn't very verbose, you'll just see the truffle prompt:

```
truffle(development)>
```

Links

Truffle Console
`bit.ly/2XIOyPo`

Migrate Contracts

As mentioned earlier, the process of compiling and deploying your contracts to the blockchain is called migration in ETH-speak. Currently, we have our blockchain up and running and a Truffle console connected to it. Before we can do anything else, we need to migrate.

At the truffle prompt, enter the following command:

```
migrate --reset
```

This will compile the contracts and deploy them to the blockchain, outputting something similar to:

```
truffle(development)> Using network 'development'.

Running migration: 1_initial_migration.js
  Deploying Migrations...
  ... 0xd1cb134769b8012a1ec95fcd40bd-
c89c13214006fc696619bc2147130947b572
  Migrations: 0x06b97e17491dbfe84493f8e86bb80600219b5309
Saving successful migration to network...
  ... 0xbf928907d-
f7d4d6553a19a0c2b65a7a180b482c9deefa396b796f12b8fe19a2c
Saving artifacts...
Running migration: 2_deploy_contracts.js
  Running step...
  Deploying FiatContract...
  ... 0x31b8177eeaaebe1d-
de7c1e622f3927ac58967f62ee7f262a026a43e521710a6b
```

```
  FiatContract: 0x41c2ee14b9b46e9dbe0a5ce18c4d8d5080b168ba
  ... 0xaea4bfd-
b72c9a336564a85e954187f74b7883c5ceeec347600172a9855a0e154
  Deploying StockRoom...
  ... 0xe57e2bc7bf2b9a54f3c0e0d942e65c105ae5c6a6a66d-
c7f2f6a93f118844e56e
  StockRoom: 0x22740ab6785e553b041ad47ab5575d244fde22fe
  Deploying ProShop...
  ... 0xfb1584f1e00573d0ae405d4dcb9524a0555f-
b9a82f78a3546887a4c117888e06
  ProShop: 0x6bf93c90df0f01d3dbbbe8aef7b3c9a3096a9ddd
Setting FiatContact address
  ... 0x8234c18b1a0d0e609d182887533ea323b767f6e7eaf82f1ea2e3cd-
cf57fcc663
Setting StockRoom Contract address
  ... 0x2238c1db87caf8efc03832ebdd6362199e42f4e86d-
d060a09918c908019162be
  ...
0x34e1929fd76d50c5c7cb1f9c4ec3a76e937b713d08189258f6a6f71942fa7312
  ... 0x6dc7086a3a0b9159100021ff75e2546c2945ba8b90eecde30b4807c-
c5cdd38a5
Saving successful migration to network...
  ... 0xd80c7dc911faaf7e11b7747e2dd66b15de8bded8d-
d3b5c51624590f888b62364
Saving artifacts...
```

Assuming all went well, you should now have the In-App Pro Shop contracts up and running on your local blockchain.

Test Contracts

It would be crazy to attempt smart contract development without unit tests. Our unit tests for the contracts are located in the top-level *test* folder of the project. We can get a quick sanity check that everything is working as expected by launching the tests from within the Truffle console.

At the truffle prompt, just run:

```
test
```

You should see output similar to the following:

```
Using network 'development'.

Setting FiatContact address
Setting StockRoom Contract address

  Contract: ItemFactory
    ✓ should not allow a user to create an Item if the SKU price
is not sent (159ms)
    ✓ should calculate the right Item price in ether (92ms)
    ✓ should allow a user to create an Item (472ms)
    ✓ should not allow a user to create a limited Item when limit
has been reached (139ms)
    ✓ should allow a user to retrieve a count of their items
    ✓ should allow a user to retrieve a list of their items
(289ms)

  Contract: ProShop
```

✓ should allow the franchise owner to check their balance in Ether (39ms)

✓ should allow the franchise owner to check their balance in the Franchise fiat currency (73ms)

✓ should not allow anyone else to check the franchise balance (84ms)

✓ should allow the franchise owner to withdraw their balance (1069ms)

✓ should allow the shop owner to check their balance in Ether (46ms)

✓ should allow the shop owner to check their balance in their Shop's fiat currency (83ms)

✓ should allow anyone to convert an Ether amount to a Shop's fiat currency (46ms)

✓ should allow the shop owner to withdraw their balance (773ms)

✓ should not allow anyone else to check the shop balance (88ms)

Contract: SKUFactory
✓ should not allow someone other than shop owner to create a SKU for a Shop (56ms)

✓ should allow a shop owner to create a SKU of an existing SKU Type for their Shop (358ms)

Contract: SKUTypeFactory
✓ should not allow someone other than shop owner to create a SKU Type for a Shop (42ms)

✓ should allow a shop owner to create a SKU Type for their Shop (295ms)

Contract: ShopFactory
✓ should allow anyone to create a shop (286ms)
✓ should allow an existing shop owner to create another shop (248ms)

✓ should allow shop owner retrieve a list of their shops
✓ should allow shop owner retrieve a shop by id (323ms)

23 passing (11s)

We'll go further into how the unit tests are coded in a later chapter. For now, suffice it to say that we can be confident the contracts are deployed and operating as expected.

Create Mock Data

Next, we want to create some mock data that the application can use when when launch it. The unit tests created their own instances of the contracts, so that data won't be visible to the application. In order to create the mock data, we will use the Truffle console to execute some Javascript that communicates with the deployed contracts.

At the truffle prompt run the following commands in order:

```
exec mock/CreateShops.js
exec mock/CreateSKUTypes.js
exec mock/CreateSKUs.js
exec mock/CreateSales.js
```

Your output should look like this:

```
truffle(development)> exec mock/CreateShops.js
Using network 'development'.

Shops created.
truffle(development)> exec mock/CreateSKUTypes.js
Using network 'development'.

SKU Types created.
truffle(development)> exec mock/CreateSKUs.js
Using network 'development'.

SKUs created.
truffle(development)> exec mock/CreateSales.js
Using network 'development'.
```

```
SHOP: 0 SKU 0 PRICE 42065163987500000
SHOP: 0 SKU 0 PRICE 42065163987500000
SHOP: 0 SKU 0 PRICE 42065163987500000
SHOP: 0 SKU 0 PRICE 42065163987500000
SHOP: 0 SKU 0 PRICE 42065163987500000
SHOP: 0 SKU 1 PRICE 16826065595000000
SHOP: 0 SKU 1 PRICE 16826065595000000
SHOP: 0 SKU 1 PRICE 16826065595000000
SHOP: 0 SKU 1 PRICE 16826065595000000
SHOP: 0 SKU 1 PRICE 16826065595000000
SHOP: 1 SKU 2 PRICE 6730426238000000
SHOP: 1 SKU 2 PRICE 6730426238000000
SHOP: 1 SKU 2 PRICE 6730426238000000
SHOP: 1 SKU 2 PRICE 6730426238000000
SHOP: 1 SKU 2 PRICE 6730426238000000
SHOP: 1 SKU 3 PRICE 13460852476000000
SHOP: 1 SKU 3 PRICE 13460852476000000
SHOP: 1 SKU 3 PRICE 13460852476000000
SHOP: 1 SKU 3 PRICE 13460852476000000
SHOP: 1 SKU 3 PRICE 13460852476000000
Sales created.
```

For grins, let's take a look at one of those scripts, to see just how easy it is to communicate with the contract from JavaScript using Truffle. Here is the content of *mock/CreateShops.js*:

```
// Create mock shops
const StockRoom = artifacts.require("./StockRoom.sol");

module.exports = async function(done){

    const shopOwner =
'0x8b7bb2c31bc7e02d84060ca87e8218cb3b57678d';
    const names = ["Barely Legal Pawn", "Fairly Regal Pawn"];
    const descs = ["Great stuff, cheap!", "Cheap stuff, pricey!"];
    const fiat = 'USD';
    let contract = await StockRoom.deployed();
    let promises = names.map( (name, idx) =>
contract.createShop(name, descs[idx], fiat, {from: shopOwner}) );
    try {
        await Promise.all(promises);
        console.log('Shops created.');
    } catch (error) {
```

```
        console.log(error.message);
    }
    done();

};
```

This script requires the *Stockroom* contract using Truffle's `arti-facts` construct. It exports an async function which Truffle Console will execute. That function hardcodes the Shop Owner's address (another reason we need to start Ganache in deterministic mode). It gets a reference to the deployed contract and then uses the contract's `createShop` function to create two Shops. That function can only be executed by the Shop Owner, so it's important we use that address when invoking the function.

Compile and Serve App

The blockchain is running, the contracts are deployed and tested, and the mock data is installed. We're ready to compile and serve the client application.

Return to the original Terminal window where you installed the project, or if you closed it, open a new one and navigate to the project folder.

The client application is built on React and uses *react-scripts* to compile and serve the application. If you've ever used *create-react-app*, this startup process will be familiar. At the system prompt, just run the following command: `npm run app:start`

The output should resemble the following:

```
> in-app-pro-shop@1.0.0 app:start /Users/cliff/Documents/in-app-
pro-shop
> react-app-rewired start

⚡ ⚡ ⚡ Overriding default Create React App Configuration! ⚡ ⚡ ⚡
Starting the development server...

Compiled successfully!

You can now view in-app-pro-shop in the browser.

  Local:            http://localhost:3000/
  On Your Network:  http://192.168.2.38:3000/
```

Note that the development build is not optimized. To create a production build, use npm run build.

Install MetaMask

The MetaMask plugin allows users to specify their Ethereum accounts and their associated private keys. Then, when they navigate to a web app that would like to use their account(s) to perform transactions on the blockchain, they are asked if they'd like to connect their account. Users will generally be using MetaMask plugin or the Brave Browser, both of which you can install from the MetaMask website.

Once you've installed the plugin, do the following:
- Click the MetaMask icon on the browser's toolbar.
- Open the Network dropdown (may show "Main Ethereum Network").
- Choose Custom RPC.
- Accept the defaults for Currency Conversion, Primary Currency, and Language.
- Scroll down to New Network.
- In the New RPC URL field, enter "`http://localhost: 7545`".
- Click the Save button.
- Make sure Private Network is now shown in the network dropdown.

Links

MetaMask
```
metamask.io
```

Add an Account

Now MetaMask knows about your network, but it still doesn't know about any accounts on it.

Remember earlier, when I mentioned that we needed to run Ganache in deterministic mode so it would create the same accounts every time? Well, not only is that important for our hard-coded accounts in mock data scripts, but we need to enter one or more of those accounts into MetaMask so we can interact with our local blockchain data.

MetaMask will have created a default account, which is useless to us. Its generated avatar is on the right side of the MetaMask window when you click the icon on your browser's toolbar. If you click that avatar, you'll see the My Accounts window. "Account 1" is the throwaway account we don't care about.

Now, do the following:

- Click the Import Account menu option.
- In your Ganache terminal, scroll back to the Private Keys it output when you started it. The first key (0) is for the Franchise Owner's account. Copy it and paste it into the Private Key field.
- Click the Import button. The My Accounts window will close and the new account will be imported as "Account 2".

- Click the hamburger menu (on the left of "Account 2"). You'll see a window with info about the account. Beside the account name is an edit (pencil icon) button. Click it and change the name to "Franchise Owner".
- Repeat all the above steps to import the second private key in Ganache's list, and name the account "Shop Owner".
- Import the third private key and name the account "Item Owner".

Open App in Browser

Now all you need to do is make sure the Shop Owner's account is selected in MetaMask, then open `http://localhost:3000/` in a new browser tab. MetaMask should ask you if In-app Pro Shop can connect to your account. Click the Connect button and the app should connect to the blockchain and display your account and shops as shown below.

Summary

You should now have a working and tested installation of In-App Pro Shop on your machine, or at least understand what it takes to make that happen. This gets all the installation of code and dependencies out of the way. You can nose around in the codebase and even fiddle with it if you'd like, before moving on.

When you're ready, move on to the next chapter, where we'll begin looking into the structure of smart contracts and their tests.

CHAPTER FOUR

Writing Contracts

We could just hop right into coding a contract and start learning about data types, functions, return values, modifiers, interfaces, etc. We will get into all those things, but going straight to that level can make it difficult to see the forest for the trees.

I know. I started there and learned several lessons the hard way.

The point of this book is not to teach every detail of Solidity from first principles. Rather, it is to impart the most important things to know about the ecosystem you're working within and how they affect your quotidian efforts. If you have a strategy before you go into battle, your likelihood of winning is greatly improved.

Constraints and Strategy

I want to begin by discussing some of the constraints on a contract. After all, when we start coding a contract, we want to know what can safely go into it.

How big can one be? Is there a limit? Should we have a strategy in mind for building our contracts, or is it OK to just treat them as a big bag of functions?

Also, contracts (like classes in an OOP language) can inherit functionality from other contracts — more than one, even! What do we need to think about in terms of inheritance structure and relationships between contracts?

Contract Size

There are plenty of ways to go about structuring the smart contracts for your Ethereum blockchain project. I'll describe how In-App Pro Shop's evolved, but the key bit of wisdom I took away from the experience is: *think small*.

When I began with this project, I added plenty of data structures, mappings, and functions that seemed like they'd eventually be useful. Ways to look up this by that, AND by the other thing. Honestly, I was just thinking ahead.

What I had failed to realize was that there is a very real limitation on the size of your contracts — the block gas limit.

Though this amount changes slowly over time and may vary between the mainnet and testnets, just remember that a transaction will not succeed if it requires more gas than the current block gas limit. Since deploying a contract is achieved via a transaction, and the more data to be written to the blockchain the more gas required, it follows that there is a hard upper limit on the size of any given contract.

Your contracts will grow bit by bit and one day, you'll go to deploy and find that you can't, due to the block gas limit. Now all you can do is cast off ballast. Your options are to remove unused functions, structures, etc., optimize necessary ones, or move them to another contract, which is no light undertaking for a number of reasons.

So, as your project evolves, write only what you need, just when it's needed, no sooner.

Links

Check Gas Limit on Mainnet
`bit.ly/2Yth2cJ`

For Ropsten Testnet
`bit.ly/2XpELOz`

Contract Architecture

Solidity has inheritable classes — called contracts — and interfaces similar to object-oriented languages like Java. If, like me, you are (or have been) an OOP developer, you're probably already thinking about how you might split your contracts into actors with clearly defined roles, responsibilities, and collaboration patterns. If so, I hate to burst your bubble, but the unique environment of the blockchain is going to work against you here.

For one thing, communication between contracts takes more gas than function calls within a single contract. Also, every separately deployed contract in your system increases the overall attack surface. Maybe you assume contract A will be the only caller to contract B because that's the way you designed it, but hackers will hit every public function of every contract you deploy, looking for a vulnerability. So there is a not-so-gentle pressure to keep it all in a single contract if at all possible.

Why then, you might ask, even have inheritable classes and interfaces if you're not going to create an architecture composed of actors that implement some sort of polymorphism?

Well, you will... after a fashion.

You'll use libraries like Open Zeppelin to imbue your contracts with functionality like role-based access, or to implement the ERC-721 interface for NFTs. To take advantage of all this pre-built goodness, you will usually inherit from their contracts. In doing so, you'll be relying on the "many eyes" principle of open source. Open Zeppelin's code for these core capabilities has been reviewed, tested, and probed by a great many developers, and so is likely much more robust than an implementation you might develop in support of your application, which itself has a completely different high-level goal.

But within a small application, there's very little need to create interfaces and separate deployable contracts for the purpose of implementing a traditional OOP architecture. Again, size, gas, and attack surface preclude this sort of thinking.

Stratification of Concerns

Whether you're an OOP developer or not, at this point, you may be thinking you could put all your code in one contract, import and extend the utility contracts you need, and be done with it. You'd be absolutely correct.

But there's still a good argument for building a contract hierarchy. You may not be implementing a classic OOP separation of concerns, but you can still stratify them.

For the In-App Pro Shop, I placed all the data structures in a base contract, extended it with a contract for implementing access control, then stacked on contracts for handling maintenance of each domain entity: Shops, SKU Types (categories), SKUs ("stock-keeping units" or item descriptions), and Items (minted tokens). The final contract at the tip of the inheritance chain dealt with withdrawal of shop and franchise balances.

When the contracts are compiled, only that final contract needs to be deployed to the blockchain. Its byte code contains the whole inheritance chain, including the specific Open Zeppelin contracts extended by the base.

Why is this better than putting it all in one source file?

- You still get the benefit of a single deployable contract.

- Shorter files are easier to navigate and comprehend in any language.
- All the data structures that the intermediate contracts use is in one place.
- You can quickly isolate and test the functionality you are working on at any given moment.

Initial Hierarchy

Throughout much of the In-App Pro Shop project's development, the inheritance hierarchy looked like the following:

```
* ERC721Full (Open Zeppelin contract for non-fungible tokens)
:
:  * AccessControl (Roles, SafeMath, pause, unpause, upgrade)
:..:
:
* ProShopBase (Structs and state related to Items and balances)
:
* ItemFactory (Factory method and event for minting new Items)
:
* ProShop (Utility methods for withdrawing balances)
```

These were simpler and more straightforward times.

Solidity contracts support multiple inheritance, so our base contract *ProShopBase* inherited from OpenZeppelin's *Roles* (role-based access control) and *ERC721Full* contracts. This gives us everything we need (that's inheritable) from a third-party standpoint and it will be inherited by all our other contracts.

The *ProShopBase* contract represents the domain model. It defines all our domain entity data structures and state variables. Contracts inheriting from it can work with whatever aspects of the contract's state they need.

We implement custom roles for System Administrator, Shop Owner, and Franchise Owner. Various functions within the system will require the user to have one of these roles in order to be executed. Therefore, the *AccessControl* contract is the first to inherit from *ProShopBase*, so that the subsequent contracts in the inheritance chain can use its functionality.

The Shop entity doesn't refer to any other entity. Accordingly, *ShopFactory* should never need to access the functionality of any of the other entity factory contracts. Its job will primarily be to create Shop entities and emit events when a Shop is created. In this initial hierarchy, it also had helper functions for looking up Shops by owner and the like as well. So *ShopFactory* inherits directly from *AccessControl*.

The remaining factory contracts are ordered in the hierarchy by what references what. SKUs reference SKU Types and Shops, so *SKUTypeFactory* inherits from *ShopFactory* and *SKUFactory* inherits from *SKUTypeFactory*. Items reference SKUs, SKU Types, and Shops, and so *ItemFactory* inherits from *SKUFactory*.

Keep in mind that all the domain entity data structures are available to all the factory contracts via their inheritance of the base *StockRoomBase* contract. This ordering was imposed in case one of the factory contracts needed to access another's functions for whatever reason. That didn't actually end up happening, but it could in your contracts, so keep it in mind when creating your linages.

Finally, the *ProShop* inherits from *ItemFactory*, and along with it all the above described functionality. It adds functions for reporting and withdrawing the Shop Owner and Franchise Owner balances. When this contract is deployed, all of the functions, data structures, and state variables defined above might as well have been written in one big contract. But the system is far easier to reason about when it is stratified in this way.

The Inevitable Bifurcation Event

If your project is ambitious enough, you'll hit that aforementioned hard ceiling and will no longer be able to deploy your contract.

It happened to me and it was a sad, sad day.

I got an "out of gas" error during the migration process, and my happy little development process screeched to a halt. The crucial thing to know is: **you're not running out of gas**. It's not that your contract requires more gas to deploy than the block gas limit. In fact it has nothing whatsoever to do with gas.

EIP-170 (an Ethereum Improvement Proposal) states:

> If block.number >= FORK_BLKNUM, then if contract creation initialization returns data with length of **more than** 0x6000 (2**14 + 2**13) bytes, contract creation fails with an out of gas error.

Apparently, Vitalik Buterin, creator of Ethereum, decided that the contract code size needed to be capped. But rather than returning a sensible message like "maximum contract code size exceeded" he just decreed that "out of gas" would be returned.

As a result, developers are likely to waste a lot of time trying to address the issue with gas-related configurations.

You'll optimize. You'll give your transaction more gas. You'll look up the current block gas limit on the mainnet and testnets and hope that you can increase it on your local blockchain in your *truffle.js* (in `networks.development.gas`):

```
module.exports = {
    networks: {
        development: {
            host: "127.0.0.1",
            port: 7545,
            from: "0xea5f1f147332e32a0dbbf25f4cbcb78d8ba879ce",
            network_id: "*",
            gas: 8000000
        }
    }
};
```

But eventually, you'll realize you have no other choice but to split the hierarchy into separate lineages, terminating in two or more deployable contracts that must talk to each other. That means they'll also need interfaces which describe their public function signatures. And they'll be more vulnerable to attack, opening a separate can of worms.

In the case of In-App Pro Shop, I split the contract into two lineages called *ProShop* and *StockRoom*.

The *ProShop* line contains the code associated with minting Items and withdrawing shop and franchise balances. It looks like this:

```
* ERC721Full (Open Zeppelin contract for non-fungible tokens)
:
:   * AccessControl (Roles, SafeMath, pause, unpause, upgrade)
:..:
:
* ProShopBase (Structs and state related to Items and balances)
:
* ItemFactory (Factory method and event for minting new Items)
:
* ProShop (Utility methods for withdrawing balances)
```

The *StockRoom* line contains the code associated with maintaining Shops, SKU Types, and SKUs.

```
* AccessControl (Roles, SafeMath pause, unpause, upgrade)
:
* StockRoomBase (Structs and state for Shops, SKU Types, and SKUs)
:
* ShopFactory (Factory method and event for new Shops)
:
* SKUTypeFactory (Factory method and event for new SKU Types)
:
* SKUFactory (Factory method and event for new SKUs)
:
* StockRoom (Utility methods for accessing contract data)
```

You'll notice the *StockRoom* contract doesn't inherit from *ERC721-Full* like *ProShop* does. That's because we only work with NFTs in the *ProShop*. *StockRoom* is concerned with all the other entities and state variables. However, both contracts need role-based access control and overflow protection for arithmetic operations, so they both inherit from *AccessControl*.

Even though the bifurcation event was an unwelcome day of refactoring, I'm still not certain that I'd advise beginning with multiple lineages by design. At least when you're starting out. I would instead recommend putting a premium on contract size, safety, and transaction cost by keeping everything in one deployed contract. Only split when absolutely necessary. Once you have some experience under your belt, understand all the security concerns, and find yourself presented with a system you're certain will encompass multiple contract lineages, then by all means, do what you have to do.

Links

EIP-170 - Contract code size limit
`bit.ly/2TEKQ6X`

Solidity Basics

As promised, having reviewed some of the constraints on size and structure, we'll now dive into some of the details of coding in Solidity. It's an easy language to pick up, and has some unique features owing to its execution environment.

For instance, since contracts are meant to hold and exchange actual currency, these capabilities are directly expressed in the language.

Not only does a contract have an Ether balance, the values of its global variables persist and can be manipulated by successive interactions with its functions. As such, they often implement state machines. That is to say, they can transition through any number of discrete named states according to certain rules. An auction contract might have a bidding state during which it accepts bids, and a closed state during which bidding is not allowed.

And since it always knows the address of the invoking account or contract, it is capable of restricting the operation of any given function to a specific address or group of addresses.

These are just a few of the qualities of Ethereum smart contracts supported by the Solidity language that make it interesting to work with. Yet it is syntactically familiar to many other languages you may know.

Version Pragma, Inheritance, and Libraries

Initially, as described in the previous section, there was only one base contract in our project, *ProShopBase*, which contained data structure and variable definitions. The next contract in the line was one which implemented role-based access control, *AccessControl*.

But after the great bifurcation event, the project was left with two contract lineages, and thus two base contracts, *ProShopBase* and *StockroomBase*. Both required access control features. So, aside from the Open Zeppelin contracts, *AccessControl* can now be considered the base custom contract in our system. It is common to all lineages.

This codebase has been updated several times along the way, as Solidity evolved. The original implementation of *AccessControl* conveniently demonstrated several key features of Solidity, so let's examine it first.

In the following excerpt from *AccessControl.sol*, note the `pragma` line at the top of the file. Solidity is a fast-evolving language, and so all contracts written in it should include this line. It defines the minimum version of the compiler that's required to interpret the contract properly. If a prior or incompatible future version of the compiler is presented this code, it will fail to compile.

```
// AccessControl.sol - partial code below...

pragma solidity ^0.4.24;
```

```
import "openzeppelin-solidity/contracts/ownership/RBAC/RBAC.sol";

contract AccessControl is RBAC {
    string public constant ROLE_SYS_ADMIN = "role/system-admin";
    string public constant ROLE_FRANCHISE_OWNER = "role/franchise-
owner";
    constructor() public {
        paused = true;
        addRole(msg.sender, ROLE_SYS_ADMIN);
        addRole(msg.sender, ROLE_FRANCHISE_OWNER);
    }
}
```

Next, we import the Open Zeppelin *RBAC* contract, which provides us with some handy functions for implementing role-based access control. The *AccessControl* contract definition then explicitly inherits from (or "extends") *RBAC* with the **is** keyword.

We declare a public constructor, which immediately makes use of an inherited *RBAC* feature, `addRole`.

The `msg.sender` variable is always present upon execution of a contract's public functions (including the constructor) and could represent a wallet address or the address of another smart contract.

If you look back at the *truffle.js* file in the previous section, under `networks.development.from`, you'll see an Ethereum address. When you deploy the contract, that's the address that shows up in the `msg.sender` property. Our constructor makes a couple of calls to the `addRole` function, giving the instantiating address the roles of Franchise Owner and System Admin.

Now, we get role-based access functionality from the *Roles* library. The refactoring of *AccessControl* to use this library gives us a good opportunity to see how library usage differs from inheritance.

```
// AccessControl.sol - Refactored - partial code below...

pragma solidity ^0.5.12;
```

```
import "openzeppelin-solidity/contracts/access/Roles.sol";

contract AccessControl {

    using Roles for Roles.Role;

    Roles.Role internal admins;
    Roles.Role internal franchise;
    Roles.Role internal shopOwners;

    constructor() public {
        paused = true; // Start paused
        admins.add(msg.sender);
        franchise.add(msg.sender);
    }
}
```

In addition to the `import` change, note that we have dropped the 'is RBAC' from the contract declaration. Instead we now have 'using Roles.Role', which tells the compiler that we want to use a custom data type (struct) called `Role` from the *Roles* library we've imported. Then we define a few `internal` variables of that type, `admins`, `franchise`, and `shopOwners`. We still give these roles to the `msg.sender` address in the constructor. It's just a slightly different syntax.

How do we make use of those roles in the system?

The Franchise and Shop Owner don't come into play until we get into some of the other contracts, but we can see the System Admin role implemented in this particular contract.

Notice that `paused` variable initialized to false in the constructor? Well, we'll want to implement the ability to toggle that, but only if the account attempting to do so has the System Admin role.

To see how that's done, let's look at a little more of the code in this contract.

Visibility

You probably noticed in the previous example that the constructor function was labeled `public`. There are four visibility specifiers in Solidity: `external`, `public`, `internal`, and `private`. Function and state variable visibility determines — as in most languages that have it — who can call a function or access the variable. As of Solidity version `0.5.0`, explicit visibility declaration is mandatory for all functions.

As you probably can tell, these four specifiers lie along a spectrum.

External Visibility

Functions labeled `external` can only be called from outside the contract, by a user's Ethereum address or another contract.

Interestingly, while you can't use `functionName()` to call an external function from within a contract, you can use `this.functionName()`.

External functions can be more efficient when they receive large arrays of data. State variables cannot be declared `external`. Also, on interface declarations, you must use the `external` specifier on all function signatures.

Public Visibility

Functions and state variables labeled `public` can be accessed from outside the contract, or from within the contract using `functionName()`.

Internal Visibility

Functions and state variables labeled `internal` can only be accessed internally, i.e., from within the contract or contracts deriving from it.

Private Visibility

Functions and state variables labeled `private` can only be accessed from within the contract they are defined in, and not by derived contracts.

Keep in mind that the blockchain is public, and all data there is readable. Visibility specifiers only control whether contracts or transactions can access the functions or state variables to which they are attached.

Modifiers

In order to determine whether the user has the System Admin role we will use a `modifier` declaration. Further, if the user has that role, there will be functions they should only be able to execute when the contract is paused, and others when it is not paused. A modifier can be used to make that determination as well.

```
// AccessControl.sol - partial code below...

contract AccessControl {

    bool public paused = false;

    modifier onlySysAdmin() {
        require(admins.has(msg.sender));
        _;
    }

    modifier whenNotPaused() {
        require(!paused);
        _;
    }

    modifier whenPaused() {
        require(paused);
        _;
    }

    function pause() public onlySysAdmin whenNotPaused {
        paused = true;
        emit ContractPaused();
    }
```

```
function unpause() public onlySysAdmin whenPaused {
    paused = false;
    emit ContractUnpaused();
}

}
```

First, notice the `onlySysAdmin` modifier declaration. This is essentially a function block that calls the inherited `checkRole` function to find out if the invoker has the System Admin role. But after that call, there is a strange-looking statement: `_;`. To understand what that underscore keyword does, you need to know how this modifier's code gets called in the first place.

Look at the definition for the `pause` function. After the `public` modifier and before the code block surrounded by curly braces, there are two further modifiers: `onlySysAdmin` and `whenNotPaused`.

The `onlySysAdmin` modifier's code isn't invoked like a regular function. Rather, it is called as a guard condition. When we call the `pause` function, the Ethereum Virtual Machine (EVM) will first call the code in `onlySysAdmin` and `whenNotPaused`. The intention is fairly obvious; we only want the System Admin to be able to execute the code in this function, and then only when the contract is not already paused. We didn't have to add parentheses to the modifiers here, but that's only because there were no arguments to pass. Modifiers can accept arguments and in that case they look like a regular function call when used.

Now that you know how the modifier code gets called, what's up with that underscore statement? It basically means "carry on, all good here." If there's a problem, we don't want to execute that line, how do we achieve that?

The next line of code after a `require` statement is only reached if the expression passed to `require` resolves to true. And if the modifier doesn't execute a `_;` line, then the code it's guarding doesn't get executed. In the case of `onlySysAdmin` we call `admins.has`, which in turn has a `require` statement that fails if the address we pass doesn't have the specified role. You can also see `require` used in our `whenPaused` and `whenNotPaused` modifiers which evaluate the state of the `paused` variable.

Function Types

Functions in Solidity can do all sorts of things. Knowing what a function actually does, we can declare them to be of a particular type, so the EVM can more efficiently handle their execution.

The primary distinction between function types is whether it reads from or modifies state.

Stateful Functions

Let's say you have a function that reads a state variable, modifies another state variable, then emits an event. This would be considered a stateful function and you don't need to add any function type to its signature. Here's a good example from *AccessControl*:

```
function upgradeContract(address _newAddress)
external onlySysAdmin whenPaused whenNotUpgraded {
    upgraded = true;
    newContractAddress = _newAddress;
    emit ContractUpgrade(_newAddress);
}
```

Its modifiers read state variables to determine if the contract is paused or upgraded, and then it sets state variables and emits an event. Definitely interacting with state.

The canonical list of things that are considered to be state-modifying are:

- Writing to state variables.
- Emitting events.
- Creating other contracts.
- Using selfdestruct.
- Sending Ether via calls.
- Calling any function not marked view or pure.
- Using low-level calls.
- Using inline assembly that contains certain opcodes.

View Functions

Now consider a function that doesn't modify state at all, but may need to read it. It would be appropriate to label it as `view`. Here's an example from *StockRoom*:

```
function convertEtherToFranchiseFiat(uint256 _amount)
external view
returns (uint256) {
    uint256 quote = getQuote("USD");
    return _amount.div(quote);
}
```

It does not otherwise modify state in any way. It calls a function `getQuote()` — which it is important to point out, does no modification of state itself, but that's it. The function implements read-only behavior with regard to state.

Pure Functions

For a function to be considered pure, it must secret itself away upon a remote mountain top for many years... Actually, it just needs to abstain from interacting with state in any way, neither reading nor writing to it. Here's another good example from *Stock-Room*:

```
function isStockRoom()
```

```
external pure returns (bool) {
    return true;
}
```

This particular function only needs to acknowledge that it is the *StockRoom* contract being called, by returning a value of `true`. It has no state-checking modifiers and references no state variables or other stateful or view functions.

In addition to not modifying state, it must not read from state, and here are the things that are considered to be state-reading:

- Reading from state variables.
- Accessing address(this).balance or <address>.balance.
- Accessing any of the members of block, tx, and msg (with the exception of msg.sig and msg.data).
- Calling any function not marked pure.
- Using inline assembly that contains certain opcodes.

Events

Another Solidity feature exhibited by our *AccessControl* contract is that it defines and emits events.

```
// AccessControl.sol - partial code below...

contract AccessControl {

    event ContractPaused();

    event ContractUnpaused();

    bool public paused = false;

    function pause() public onlySysAdmin whenNotPaused {
        paused = true;
        emit ContractPaused();
    }

    function unpause() public onlySysAdmin whenPaused {
        paused = false;
        emit ContractUnpaused();
    }

}
```

In the `pause` and `unpause` functions above, now shown in their entirety, note the `emit` statements.

Above these functions, you'll see the `event` declarations, which in the case of `ContractPaused` and `ContractUnpaused` take no arguments. Soon, we'll see an example of event with arguments.

In the case of these two events, we're just notifying whoever may care that the `paused` state of our contract has changed.

When something happens on the blockchain and a contract emits an `event`, clients out in the world can be notified simply by listening for it. We'll see how that happens in a later chapter.

Structures and State

In the following extract from the *ProShopBase* contract, we define the state variables and the single data structure that the ProShop lineage refers to and manipulates.

```
// ProShopBase.sol - partial code below...

contract ProShopBase is ERC721Full, AccessControl {

    Item[] public items;

    mapping (uint256 => uint256[]) public skuItems;

    mapping (uint256 => uint256[]) public shopItems;

    mapping (address => uint256[]) public ownedItems;

    mapping (uint256 => uint256) public shopBalances;

    uint256 public franchiseBalance;

    uint256 public franchiseFeePercent;

    struct Item {

        // Owner of the item
        address owner;

        // The shop this item belongs to
        uint256 shopId;

        // The id of this item
```

```
    uint256 itemId;

    // Id of SKU of this item
    uint256 skuId;

    // Has the item been consumed?
    bool consumed;
  }

}
```

State variables are values held in the contract which can be altered by the contract's functions. As such, they represent the state of the contract at any given time.

The first variable declared is the publicly accessible `items` array, which holds instances of the `Item` struct, defined at the bottom of the contract. An Item is the ERC721 NFT that the *ItemFactory* contract mints. It tracks the Ethereum address of its owner, the ID of the Shop that minted it, its own unique ID, the ID of the SKU that describes it, and a boolean flag that indicates if it has been consumed. Items can be consumable (think a magic potion that has been drunk, and is no longer usable).

After the items array, we define a few mappings. Mappings are akin to associative arrays in other languages. They are a collection of key/value pairs.

The `skuItems` mapping has a key that is a `uint256` (256-bit unsigned integer), and a value that is an array of `uint256`s. It maps a `skuId` to all the Items that have that `skuId`. This allows us to look up all the Items of a particular SKU.

The `shopItems` mapping has a key that is a `uint256`, and a value that is an array of `uint256`s. It maps a `shopId` to all the Items that have that `shopId`. This allows us to look up all the Items minted by a particular Shop.

The `ownedItems` mapping has a key that is an Ethereum address, and a value that is an array of `uint256`s. It maps an address to all the Items that have that `owner`. This allows us to find all the Items owned by a given user.

The `shopBalances` mapping has a key that is a `uint256`, and a value that is also a `uint256`. It maps a `shopId` to its current Ether balance. This allows us to determine how much of the contract's balance is owed to a given Shop.

Next, we define a `uint256` called `franchiseBalance`. This allows us to determine how much of the contract's balance is owed to the franchise owner. After that another `UINT256` called `franchiseFeePercent` represents the percentage of each sale that goes to the franchise owner.

The *StockRoom* contract declares considerably more structures and state variables, but this should give you a good overview of the basics.

Reference Types and Data Location

Data types which may be of variable length (`string`, `array`, `struct`, `mapping`) are called "reference types" and they present a challenge to the EVM. They might contain large amounts of data, and could need to be copied or stored when being operated upon. Solidity now requires explicit directions about the data location for such types, even in cases where there is only one valid data location.

The available data locations are `storage`, `memory`, and `calldata`. They must be specified for function arguments, variable declarations, and return values.

What, you may ask, are the ramifications of my choice of data location, in those cases where I do have a choice?

It all comes down to whether a copy of the data is made or if a reference to the data is used.

Let's look at some examples.

```
// StockRoom - partial code below...

function getShop(uint256 _shopId)
   external
   view
   returns (
      address,
      uint256,
      string memory,
      string memory,
```

```
      string memory) {
    require(_shopId < shops.length);
    Shop memory shop = shops[_shopId];
    return (
        shop.owner,
        shop.shopId,
        shop.name,
        shop.description,
        shop.fiat
    );
}
```

In the above function, the `string` arguments being returned are marked with the `memory` data location. In the body of the function, we retrieve a `Shop` struct to a `memory` data location. In the body of the function, the following operation is performed:

```
Shop memory shop = shops[_shopId];
```

The `shops` array is as state variable, and as such is located in `storage`. By assigning it to a local variable located in `memory`, a copy will be made. The same would be true if the value were being assigned from `calldata`, which is to say, from an argument passed in from a function call.

Here we want to return from `memory` instead of directly from `storage` because it is more performant. And although it doesn't happen in this case, if we wished to make changes to the data before returning it, making a copy to `memory` first would keep us from modifying the original data in `storage`.

```
// SkuTypeFactory - partial code below...

function createSKUType(
    uint256 _shopId,
    string calldata _name,
    string calldata _desc
)
    external
```

```
    whenNotPaused
    onlyShopOwner(_shopId)
    returns(uint256)
{
    // Content omitted...
}
```

Above is an `external` function `getShop` that takes a couple of `string` arguments. Although `calldata` is the only valid location for `string` argument in an `external` function, it must still be specified.

Finally, though we don't have examples in this codebase, making an assignment from one `memory` variable to another creates a reference rather than a copy, so changes to one will be reflected in the other. This is also the case when copying from one local `storage` variable to another.

Libraries Revisited

With Solidity, there is more than one way to reuse code, whether from other projects or within your own. We've seen how inheritance works, now let's turn our attention to libraries.

For instance, Open Zeppelin's *SafeMath* is implemented as a library rather than a contract. This small collection of functions helps us avoid overflow errors (which are a well-known attack vector) in our contracts by wrapping Solidity's arithmetic operations.

As with inheritance, we first need to `import` the file containing the library code. But we don't extend it with the `is` keyword in our contract declaration. Instead, we reference it in the body of the contract.

Since both contract lineages in our system share *AccessControl* as a base contract, we can import and use *SafeMath* there, making it available throughout our system.

```
// AccessControl.sol - partial code below...
import "openzeppelin-solidity/contracts/access/Roles.sol";
import "openzeppelin-solidity/contracts/math/SafeMath.sol";

contract AccessControl {

    using SafeMath for uint256;

}
```

Importing is done in the usual way, but the `using/for` keyword construct is the important part. It's not the only way to use libraries, but it's certainly an interesting one.

The syntax is: `using [library] for [type].`

This will add the functions of the library to the specified type, in our case, `uint256`. Alternatively, we could use `*` to add the functions to *any* type.

How does this affect the way we write arithmetic operations with `uint256` variables? Let's have a look.

Below is a snippet of code from the `createItem` function of the *ItemFactory* contract. It calculates the franchise fee and the Shop's net amount when a sale is made. The variable `msg.value` is the amount of ETH that was passed into the function and `franchise-FeePercent` is a number from 0 to 100 (3 by default).

```
// Calculate and store the franchise fee
uint256 franchiseFee = uint256(
    msg.value
    .div(100)
    .mul(franchiseFeePercent)
);
franchiseBalance = franchiseBalance.add(franchiseFee);

// Calculate and store the Shop's net sale amount
uint256 shopNetSale = msg.value.sub(franchiseFee);
shopBalances[_shopId] = shopBalances[_shopId].add(shopNetSale);
```

Note that the calculations are not used with the standard arithmetic operators (`+`,`-`, `*`, `/`), but instead using the functions `add`, `sub`, `mul` and `div`. Those were added to the uint256 type by *SafeMath*.

If an overflow were to happen during one of those operations using the standard operators, the value would just "wrap around" (from maximum to zero or vise versa), which is — in almost every case — not what you want.

Hackers will take advantage of that if they can. Even if isn't a hack, your contract will end up in an unexpected, most likely undesirable state.

By using *SafeMath*, in the case of an overflow, the entire transaction is reverted and no change is made to the contract state.

It's a worthwhile exercise to review what the library actually does and how it is structured.

```
pragma solidity ^0.5.0;

/**
 * @dev Wrappers over Solidity's arithmetic operations with
 * added overflow checks.
 *
 * Arithmetic operations in Solidity wrap on overflow. This
 * can easily result in bugs, because programmers usually
 * assume that an overflow raises an error, which is the
 * standard behavior in high level programming languages.
 *
 * `SafeMath` restores this intuition by reverting the
 * transaction when an operation overflows.
 *
 * Using this library instead of the unchecked operations
 * eliminates an entire class of bugs, so it's recommended
 * to use it always.
 */
library SafeMath {

    /**
     * @dev Returns the addition of two unsigned integers,
     * reverting on overflow.
     *
     * Counterpart to Solidity's `+` operator.
     *
     * Requirements:
     * - Addition cannot overflow.
     */
    function add(uint256 a, uint256 b)
        internal
```

```
        pure
        returns (uint256)
    {

        uint256 c = a + b;
        require(c >= a, "SafeMath: addition overflow");

        return c;
    }

    /**
     * @dev Returns the subtraction of two unsigned integers,
     * reverting on overflow (when the result is negative).
     *
     * Counterpart to Solidity's `-` operator.
     *
     * Requirements:
     * - Subtraction cannot overflow.
     */
    function sub(uint256 a, uint256 b)
        internal
        pure
        returns (uint256)
    {
        require(b <= a, "SafeMath: subtraction overflow");
        uint256 c = a - b;

        return c;
    }

    /**
     * @dev Returns the multiplication of two unsigned integers,
     * reverting on overflow.
     *
     * Counterpart to Solidity's `*` operator.
     *
     * Requirements:
     * - Multiplication cannot overflow.
     */
    function mul(uint256 a, uint256 b)
        internal
        pure
        returns (uint256)
    {
        // Gas optimization: this is cheaper than requiring
        // 'a' not being zero, but the benefit is lost if 'b'
```

```
        // is also tested.
        if (a == 0) {
            return 0;
        }

        uint256 c = a * b;
        require(c / a == b, "SafeMath: multiplication overflow");

        return c;
    }

    /**
     * @dev Returns the integer division of two unsigned integers.
     * Reverts on division by zero. The result is rounded towards
     * zero.
     *
     * Counterpart to Solidity's `/` operator. Note: this function
     * uses a `revert` opcode (leaves remaining gas untouched)
     * while Solidity uses an invalid opcode to revert (consuming
     * all remaining gas).
     *
     * Requirements:
     * - The divisor cannot be zero.
     */
    function div(uint256 a, uint256 b)
        internal
        pure
        returns (uint256)
    {
        // Solidity only automatically asserts when dividing by 0
        require(b > 0, "SafeMath: division by zero");
        uint256 c = a / b;
        // There is no case in which this doesn't hold…
        // assert(a == b * c + a % b);

        return c;
    }

    /**
     * @dev Returns remainder of dividing two unsigned integers.
     * (unsigned integer modulo), reverts when dividing by zero.
     *
     * Counterpart to Solidity's `%` operator. This function uses
     * `Revert` opcode leaves remaining gas untouched while
     * Solidity uses an invalid opcode to revert (consuming all
```

```
 * remaining gas).
 *
 * Requirements:
 * - The divisor cannot be zero.
 */
function mod(uint256 a, uint256 b)
    internal
    pure
    returns (uint256)
{
    require(b != 0, "SafeMath: modulo by zero");
    return a % b;
}
}
```

Links

Solidity Library Docs
`bit.ly/32rtuw4`

Interfaces

Another way that we can access functionality implemented by other contracts is by invoking their functions directly. Be it ours or someone else's, if it has a function marked `public` or `external`, we can invoke it from our own contracts.

In order to interact with another contract in this way, we need two things to do that: an interface and an address.

As with most other languages that include them, an interface in Solidity is a partial or complete list of the accessible function signatures of a given contract. If we only need to invoke one function on the target contract, then we need only include that function's signature in the interface. When our contract invokes a functions on another contract, it needs only to know the arguments and their types as well as the return values and their types. And yes, you read that correctly; "return values" plural. A function in Solidity can return multiple values. More on that to come, in the section on testing contracts.

We have a handy example within our own project of how to invoke functions on another contract via its address and an interface. The *ProShop* contract needs to communicate with the *Stock-Room* contract to — among other things — get the current price in ETH for a given SKU. Here's the salient part of the *StockRoomInterface*:

```
// StockRoomInterface.sol - partial code below...

interface StockRoomInterface {

    /**
     * @notice get an SKU's price in Ether
     */
    function getPriceInEther(uint256 _skuId)
        external
        view
        returns (uint256);

}
```

As you can see, we use the keyword `interface` to tell the compiler that we're only interested in function signatures here. There'll be no constructor or function bodies. Earlier versions of Solidity allowed you to do this same thing with `contract`, and it didn't mind that there were no function bodies.

In order to communicate with the *StockRoom* contract, we also need to know its address. The *ProShopBase* contract includes a state variable that stores the address of the *StockRoom* contract:

```
// ProShopBase.sol - partial code below...

StockRoomInterface internal stockRoom;
```

When the contracts are deployed, *ProShop* is apprised of the *StockRoom* address by the migration script by way of its setStockRoomContractAddress function:

```
// ProShop.sol - partial code below...

/**
 * @notice Set the address of the StockRoom contract
 */
function setStockRoomContractAddress(address _address)
    external onlySysAdmin
{
```

```
StockRoomInterface candidate = StockRoomInterface(_address);

// Verify that we have the appropriate address
require(candidate.isStockRoom());

// Set the new contract address
stockRoom = candidate;
}
```

Note that only the System Administrator address can invoke the function. We don't want just anyone calling this function! We also check that the address passed in is actually an instance of the *StockRoom* contract by attempting to invoke its `isStockRoom` function. Having an identity checking function like this is highly recommended. Later, when we look at the third-party *FiatContract* interface and how we set its address on *StockRoom,* you'll see how difficult it can be to verify a contract address when such a method doesn't exist.

Now that *ProShop* has an interface and an address for *StockRoom,* it can invoke functions defined in the interface on that address. In the *ItemFactory* contract's `createItem` function, we need to check the price of a SKU so that we can be sure that enough ETH has been passed in.

```
// ItemFactory.sol - partial code below...

require(msg.value == stockRoom.getPriceInEther(_skuId));
```

Checks, Effects, Interactions

Let's jump into a another function that deals with Ether and see how subtly a vulnerability can manifest itself.

As code goes, this is rather simple, but there are plenty of things that can go wrong in a smart contract and hackers are continually uncovering more. Therefore, when handling currency, we need to be extremely careful about it and not be fooled by apparent simplicity.

In the following excerpt from the *ProShop* contract, we're allowing the Shop Owner to withdraw their Shop's balance, and emitting an event when that happens. This code is correct, but a seemingly inconsequential change in the order of operations could prove devastating.

```solidity
// ProShop.sol - partial code below...

pragma solidity ^0.5.12;

import "./ItemFactory.sol";

contract ProShop is ItemFactory {

    event ShopBalanceWithdrawn(uint256 shopId, uint256 amount);

    function withdrawShopBalance(uint256 _shopId)
        external
        whenNotPaused
        onlyShopOwner(_shopId)
```

```
    {
        uint256 amount = shopBalances[_shopId];
        require(amount > 0 && address(this).balance >= amount);
        shopBalances[_shopId] = 0;
        msg.sender.transfer(amount);
        emit ShopBalanceWithdrawn(_shopId, amount);
    }
}
```

When sales are made, the *ProShop* contract accumulates the incoming Ether in its `balance` property. The onus is on us to keep track of how that accumulating value should be split between the Franchise Owner and all the Shop Owners.

Previously in the section on libraries, we saw how that split was performed safely using *SafeMath*. Recall that for each sale, the Shop's share is added to the value in the contract's `shopBalances` array, at the index for the Shop's unique ID.

For the Shop Owner to make a withdrawal, we must invoke the `withdrawShopBalance` function on the *ProShop* contract. It takes a Shop ID as its single argument, and is declared with modifiers that identify it as being callable only from external sources (not from within the contract itself), when the contract is not paused, and only if the caller's address is the owner of the given Shop.

The first thing this function does is retrieve the value in `shop-Balances` for the Shop represented by `_shopId`. As a side note, it is idiomatic to name Solidity function arguments using a leading underscore, to distinguish them from local or contract state variables.

Next, we need to be certain that the Shop has a balance, and that the contract actually has that amount available. If we've managed the accounting properly, the contract should always have exactly the sum of the Franchise's balance and those of all the Shops. But as a precaution we still need to check for the expected amount being available.

Since we have the Shop balance in a local variable, we now set the value in the `shopBalances` array to 0. Then we transfer the amount to the Shop Owner's address by calling `msg.sender.-transfer` with the amount we retrieved from the array before zeroing it.

Finally, we emit a `ShopBalanceWithdrawn` event, passing the Shop ID and the amount, so listening clients will be aware that the transaction has taken place.

Reflecting on this code, you might think we should technically do the transfer *before* zeroing the account balance.

However, that `msg.sender` address *could* be another contract — an evil one — which could respond to the transfer by calling *back* into our contract's `withdrawShopBalance` function before returning. It would appear that the Shop still had the same balance, and we would happily initiate the transfer, *again*. The process would repeat until the entire contract balance was drained. This is called the "reentrancy" vulnerability.

Consequently, we should follow the "check-effects-interactions" pattern whenever we might be interacting with another contract. Perform all required sanity checks first, followed by any state-changing effects, and finally any interactions with external contracts. This protects us, in this case, from reentrancy attacks. We can rest comfortably because if the transfer fails, the function will revert and none of the state changes will take place, nor will an event be emitted.

Links

Check-effects-interactions pattern
`bit.ly/2FQloUd`

Trusting in Oracles

What happens if your contract needs to find out something that's not on the blockchain? Like, for instance, the current price of Ether in USD?

This turned out to be a significant hurdle for the In-App Pro Shop project. Recall, we want to set Shop prices in a relatively stable fiat currency so that the owner doesn't have to adjust them whenever the price of Ether soars or plummets. So, when someone purchases a $5 magic sword from your Shop, how much Ether do they need to pass into the `ItemFactory.createItem` function?

When we talked about constraints earlier in this chapter, we didn't touch on this one, but it's a doozy; *an Ethereum smart contract has no access whatsoever to the world outside the blockchain.*

It can't just connect to a cryptocurrency exchange and look up the going price of Ether. And it'd be naive to just expect the customer to pass in the appropriate amount of Ether when making a purchase. The honor system doesn't work on the Internet. That's a considerable hamstring to our project.

Knowing what you know about Ethereum thus far, how would you solve this problem? It's a worthwhile exercise to just close your eyes and take a moment to think it through.

How Oracles Work

If the contract cannot query the Internet, then the Internet must inform the contract.

The desire to have our contract know some piece of recent information from the Internet can be sated by having an external process which gets that data and invokes a contract function to set one or more state variables. We could run that process on a regular basis or just trigger it occasionally when some event occurs.

In the world of blockchain, such a process is called an "oracle."

Our specific case requires an oracle to provide our contract with recent conversion rates for Ether to various fiat currencies.

What would be involved in building such an oracle?

- **Getting the data.** It could come from any number of places, such as the CryptoCompare API.
- **Trusting the oracle.** The address invoking the update function must be a trusted one.
- **Periodic updates.** The freshness of the contract data is limited by the period between updates.
- **Updates cost money.** Each function invocation that sets data on the contract incurs a gas cost.

Finding the data is not a problem. We have role-based access functionality, so we could easily ensure that only a trusted party is updating the contract. We would have to determine a reasonable update frequency that balances the desire for freshness with the associated cost of updates.

Also, how many fiat currencies do we want to support? The more data we push into the contract the more expensive the update will be, whether we do a single function call with all the data or a separate calls for each currency pair.

At this point, we know that we're going to need a mechanism for repeatedly fetching Ether conversion rates and passing them to our contract. That process will require an Ethereum address with a continually available balance, so that the transactions it sends will succeed. That process will also require hosting which will probably have its own associated cost.

The In-App Pro Shop has been designed as a franchise operation, were the franchise owner takes a configurable cut of every sale made by every shop (3% by default). The system was built with this facility as a proof of concept for how a contract could provide a service and create a revenue stream. That revenue could be used to fund the ongoing operation of the oracle, potentially making it self-sustaining.

Links

CryptoCompare API
`bit.ly/2NsUxDV`

Does This Exist Already?

We have a general idea of what we'd need to build to support this exchange rate functionality. But before we go off and build it, we should survey the prior art. Surely this isn't the first smart contract that has needed to know the current price of Ether in some fiat currency, right?

Turns out there is ready-made solution out there.

Fiat Contract was created by Hunter Long and provides Ether prices in USD, EUR, and GBP. Ideally there would be support for more fiat currencies, but that would entail higher transaction costs and likely less frequent updates.

It has been updated hourly for nearly two years. There was at least one period when its funds bottomed out and were not renewed for awhile. However, there is a donation address, which funds the oracle's operation.

Getting quotes from Fiat Contract is easy. Here's an example from the official website:

```solidity
pragma solidity ^0.4.15;

// FiatContract interface
contract FiatContract {
  function ETH(uint _id) constant returns (uint256);
  function USD(uint _id) constant returns (uint256);
  function EUR(uint _id) constant returns (uint256);
  function GBP(uint _id) constant returns (uint256);
  function updatedAt(uint _id) constant returns (uint);
```

```
}


// Example contract calling FiatContract
contract Example {

    FiatContract public price;
    event NewPayment(address sender, uint256 amount);

    function Example() {
        price = FiatContract(
            0x8055d0504666e2B6942BeB8D6014c964658Ca591
        );
    }

    // returns $5.00 USD in ETH wei.
    function FiveETHUSD()
        constant
        returns (uint256)
    {
        // returns $0.01 ETH wei
        uint256 ethCent = price.USD(0);
        // $0.01 * 500 = $5.00
        return ethCent * 500;
    }

    function DoCall()
        external
        payable
        returns (string)
    {
        require(msg.value==FiveETHUSD());
        NewPayment(msg.sender, msg.value);
        return "you paid $5.00 USD!!!";
    }

}
```

First a contract is defined with the function signatures of the Fiat Contract. In more recent versions of Solidity, we would use the `interface` keyword instead of `contract` for the purposes of defining the interface. Also, the functions defined are only those we need to call as a client of the contract, not the ones that the oracle would use to update Fiat Contract's state variables.

In the `Example` contract, we define a stare variable `price` of type `FiatContract`, referring to the interface. In the constructor, we set `price` to a reference to the contract at the mainnet address where FiatContract is actually deployed. A function called `Five-ETHUSD` returns the current amount of ETH that equates to five dollars USD. Finally, the `DoCall` function is able to require a payment of five dollars USD in ETH with a simple `require` expression.

Upon discovering Fiat Contract, I had to decide whether to accept a dependency on it or to build and support similar functionality myself. That was a tough decision. What happens if Fiat Contract's oracle goes broke? I could fund it by donation. What happens if the oracle goes dark? The donations fund transactions, but surely there's a cost associated with hosting and running the oracle somewhere.

The transaction history of Fiat Contract and of its oracle's address show no shady business over the couple of years it has operated. It doesn't seem like Hunter Long will pull a fast one on us anytime soon by pulling out all the oracle donations and making off to Las Vegas. But will it always be operating? Will it eventually become too bothersome for him to maintain?

Ultimately, my decision to build on Fiat Contract didn't involve trust in the operator at all. The contract itself is open source. So as long as I provided a facility in my own contract for updating its address of Fiat Contract, I could always just deploy a copy and update it with my own oracle.

For the purposes of testing locally and on testnets, I copied the contract into my own *contracts* folder, created an interface for it and have the migration script populate it with some dummy data. So that the *StockRoom* contract will be able to get price quotes, the migration script sets the address of the Fiat Contract to be the deployed address of my own copy. For mainnet deployment, we would have the migration script set the address of the real contract on *StockRoom* and skip the dummy data population step.

Links

Fiat Contract
fiatcontract.com

Fiat Contract Transaction History
bit.ly/2KVuCmb

Fiat Contract Oracle Transaction History
bit.ly/2xsu92b

Complete Contract Suite

So far, we've seen excerpts from a few contracts for the purpose of expounding on one feature or another of the Solidity language. With these introductions to the basics out of the way, it I think it will now be worthwhile to review the contracts in their entirety.

There are two lineages, terminating in separate deployed contracts — *StockRoom* and *ProShop*. Separately, there is *FiatContract* and *FiatContractInterface*, which are included in our repository for test deployment.

Keep in mind that this is a working prototype, but a real-world implementation would want to make customizations.

For instance, it demonstrates a franchise system, wherein multiple Shop Owners create and populate their own shops. When they make sales, a franchise fee is taken out of the amount, with the net going to the Shop Owner. A company that makes games might want to create a Shop for each game might not want take out a franchise fee. That could be achieved by simply setting the `franchiseFeePercent` to 0 in the *ProShop* constructor. Or they could remove all traces of the franchise owner concept from the contract suite.

Another thing that needs some love is the SKU (shopkeeping unit), which holds the information that describes a minted Item, the actual ERC-721 token that a customer will own. Currently, the system stops short of adding unique features for each minted Item.

This is by design, since every development team will likely devise a different approach to making their tokens unique. Crypto-Kitties does this by having a `uint256` number called `genes` that is a bitmap of various traits. The algorithm is used to generate the `genes` the for a given kitty ensures certain traits are more common or rare than others and that the combination of traits is unique.

Uniqueness and provable rarity drive collectibility. In this current prototype, every magic sword sold by a Shop would be equivalent. Rarity is supported, by setting a SKU's `limited` property to `true` and its `limit` to some number. The Shop will only be able to mint that number of Items of the particular SKU. However support for unique features on each minted Item is left as an exercise to the implementer.

The Shared Base Contract

Both the *Stockroom* and *ProShop* lineages have *AccessControl* as a base contract.

As a first order of business, *AccessControl* imports the Open Zeppelin *Roles* and *SafeMath* contracts, for adding role-based access and overflow protection for arithmetic operations.

In the constructor, we add couple of roles to the address that deployed the contract: `admins` and `franchise.` These roles could be assigned to separate addresses and in a real-world implementation, I would highly recommend doing so. In that scenario, only the `admins` role would be assigned to the deployer address. Then a `setFranchiseOwner` function that had the `onlySysAdmin` modifier would be used by the deployer to add the `franchise` role to a different Ethereum address. The address with the `franchise` role can only check and withdraw the franchise balance. The address with the `admins` role can only perform maintenance operations.

Another interesting thing to note is that the `onlyShopOwner` modifier is not declared in this contract alongside the other modifiers. This is fallout of the bifurcation event that was discussed earlier in the Constraints and Strategy section of this chapter. The Shop Owner addresses are stored in the *StockRoom* contract, which means any function in that linage has access to the data as a state variable. However, the *ProShop* contract must query the *StockRoom* contract to find that information. This means that the `onlyShop-Owner` modifier must be written differently for the two contracts, and so is implemented in *StockRoomBase* and *ProShopBase*.

AccessControl.sol

```
pragma solidity ^0.5.12;

import "openzeppelin-solidity/contracts/access/Roles.sol";
import "openzeppelin-solidity/contracts/math/SafeMath.sol";

/**
 * @title AccessControl
 * Role-based access control and related functions,
 * function modifiers, and events
 */
contract AccessControl {

    using SafeMath for uint256;
    using Roles for Roles.Role;

    Roles.Role internal admins;
    Roles.Role internal franchise;
    Roles.Role internal shopOwners;

    /**
     * Constructor. Sets msg.sender as system admin by default
     */
    constructor() public {
        paused = true; // Start paused
        admins.add(msg.sender);
        franchise.add(msg.sender);
    }

    /**
     * @dev event emitted when contract is upgraded
     */
    event ContractUpgrade(address newContract);

    /**
     * @dev event emitted when contract is paused
     */
```

```
event ContractPaused();

/**
 * @dev event emitted when contract is un-npaused
 */
event ContractUnpaused();

/**
 * @dev has the contract has been upgraded?
 */
bool public upgraded = false;

/**
 * @dev is the contract is paused?
 */
bool public paused = false;

/**
 * Set if contract is broken and an upgrade is required
 */
address public newContractAddress;

/**
 * @dev modifier to scope access to system administrator
 */
modifier onlySysAdmin() {
    require(admins.has(msg.sender));
_;
}

/**
 * @dev modifier to scope access to franchise owner
 */
modifier onlyFranchiseOwner() {
    require(franchise.has(msg.sender));
    _;
}

/**
 * @dev Modifier to make a function
 * callable only when the contract
 * is not paused.
 */
modifier whenNotPaused() {
    require(!paused);
```

```solidity
        _;
}

/**
 * @dev Modifier to make a function
 * callable only when the contract
 * is paused.
 */
modifier whenPaused() {
    require(paused);
    _;
}

/**
 * Called by a system administrator to mark the
 * smart contract as upgraded, in case there is
 * a serious breaking bug. This method stores the
 * new contract address and emits an event to that
 * effect. Clients of the contract should update to
 * the new contract address upon receiving this event.
 * This contract will remain paused indefinitely
 * after such an upgrade.
 *
 * @param _newAddress address of new contract
 */
function upgradeContract(address _newAddress)
    external onlySysAdmin whenPaused whenNotUpgraded
{
    upgraded = true;
    newContractAddress = _newAddress;
    emit ContractUpgrade(_newAddress);
}

/**
 * @dev called by the system administrator
 * to pause, triggers stopped state
 */
function pause()
    public onlySysAdmin whenNotPaused
{
    paused = true;
    emit ContractPaused();
}

/**
```

```
    * @dev called by the system administrator
    * to un-pause, returns to normal state
    */
function unpause()
    public onlySysAdmin whenPaused
{
    paused = false;
    emit ContractUnpaused();
}
}
```

The StockRoom Lineage

The purpose of the *Stockroom* contract is to manage maintenance of Shops, SKU Types, SKUs, and their relationships.

A Shop is created by a Shop Owner (represented by their Ethereum address). The Shop Owner then categorizes the types of things they'll be selling by creating SKU Types. SKUs (shopkeeping units) are descriptions of the things to be sold, and are associated with a certain SKU Type.

Each SKU Type and SKU is associated with a specific Shop. Shops are associated with a certain Shop Owner. One-to-one associations are supported with ID references in the `Shop`, `SKUType`, and `SKU` data structures. One-to-many associations are supported with mappings such as `shopToOwner`, `ownerShops`, `shopSKUTypes`, `skuTypeSKUs`, and `shopSKUS`.

This lineage is basically a tower of factories, one for each of the above identified types, with a base contract defining its state variables and data structures, and a top level contract that provides a number of lookup and maintenance functions.

StockRoomBase.sol

```
pragma solidity ^0.5.12;

import "./AccessControl.sol";
import "./FiatContractInterface.sol";
```

```
/**
 * @title StockRoomBase
 * Defines collections, mappings, and structs for the
 * StockRoom side of the In-game Pro Shop System
 */
contract StockRoomBase is AccessControl {

    FiatContractInterface internal fiatContract;

    /**
     * @dev modifier to scope access to owner of given shop
     */
    modifier onlyShopOwner(uint256 _shopId) {
        address owner = shopToOwner[_shopId];
        require(msg.sender == owner);
        _;
    }

    /**
     * @notice All of the Shops
     */
    Shop[] public shops;

    /**
     * @notice All of the SKU Types
     */
    SKUType[] public skuTypes;

    /**
     * @notice All of the SKUs
     */
    SKU[] public skus;

    /**
     * @dev Mapping of Shop ID to Owner Address
     */
    mapping (uint256 => address) public shopToOwner;

    /**
     * @dev Mapping of Owner Address to list of owned Shops
     */
    mapping (address => uint256[]) public ownedShops;

    /**
```

```solidity
 * @dev Mapping of Shop ID to SKU Type list
 */
mapping (uint256 => uint256[]) public shopSKUTypes;

/**
 * @dev Mapping of SKU Type ID to SKU list
 */
mapping (uint256 => uint256[]) public skuTypeSKUs;

/**
 * @dev Mapping of Shop ID to SKU list
 */
mapping (uint256 => uint256[]) public shopSKUs;

/**
 * @notice Structure of a Pro Shop
 */
struct Shop {

    // Owner of the item
    address owner;

    // The id of this shop
    uint256 shopId;

    // Name of the item
    string name;

    // Description of the shop
    string description;

    // Fiat currency for prices
    string fiat;
}

/**
 * @notice the attributes of an item
 */
struct SKUType {

    // ID of the Shop this SKU Type belongs to
    uint256 shopId;

    // ID of the SKU Type
    uint256 skuTypeId;
```

```
    // Name of the SKU Type
    string name;

    // Description of the SKU Type (optional)
    string description;
}

/**
 * @notice Structure of a Pro Shop SKU (Shopkeeping Unit)
 */
struct SKU {

    // The shop this SKU belongs to
    uint256 shopId;

    // The id of this SKU
    uint256 skuId;

    // Type of the SKU
    uint256 skuTypeId;

    // Price of the SKU
    uint256 price;

    // Name of the item
    string name;

    // Description of the SKU
    string description;

    // Can it be consumed (used up)
    bool consumable;

    // Is there a limit to the number of Items that can
    // be minted from this SKU?
    bool limited;

    // If limited, what is the maximum number that
    // can be created?
    uint256 limit;

    }

}
```

ShopFactory.sol

```solidity
pragma solidity ^0.5.12;

import "./StockRoomBase.sol";

/**
 * @title ShopFactory
 * Defines functions and events
 * related to management of Shops
 */
contract ShopFactory is StockRoomBase {

    /**
     * @dev emitted upon creation of a shop
     * @return uint256 shopId
     */
    event NewShop(
        address indexed owner,
        uint256 shopId,
        string name
    );

    /**
     * @notice Create a Shop
     */
    function createShop(
        string calldata _name,
        string calldata _desc,
        string calldata _fiat
    )
        external whenNotPaused
        returns (uint256)
    {
        // Get Shop ID and owner address
        uint256 shopId = shops.length;
        address owner = msg.sender;

        // Create and store Shop
        shops.push(Shop(owner, shopId, _name, _desc, _fiat));

        // Map Shop ID to owner address
        shopToOwner[shopId] = owner;
```

```
        // Add Shop ID to Owner's Shops list
        ownedShops[owner].push(shopId);

        // Give the owner the ROLE_SHOP_OWNER role
        if (!shopOwners.has(owner))shopOwners.add(owner);

        // Send an event with the name of the new shop
        emit NewShop(owner, shopId, _name);

        // Return the new Shop ID
        return shopId;
    }

}
```

SKUTypeFactory.sol

```solidity
pragma solidity ^0.5.12;

import "./ShopFactory.sol";

/**
 * @title SKUTypeFactory
 * @notice Defines functions and events related to
 * management of SKU Types (Shopkeeping Units)
 */
contract SKUTypeFactory is ShopFactory {

    /**
     * @notice emitted upon the creation of a SKU Type
     */
    event NewSKUType(
        uint256 indexed shopId,
        uint256 skuTypeId,
        string name
    );

    /**
     * @notice Create a SKU Type for a Shop
     * @dev Can only be run by the shop owner
     */
    function createSKUType(
        uint256 _shopId,
```

```
                string calldata _name,
                string calldata _desc
        )
                external whenNotPaused onlyShopOwner(_shopId)
                returns(uint256)
        {
                // Get SKU Type ID
                uint256 skuTypeId = skuTypes.length;

                // Create and store SKU Type
                skuTypes.push(SKUType(_shopId, skuTypeId, _name, _desc));

                // Add SKU Type to Shop's SKU Type list
                shopSKUTypes[_shopId].push(skuTypeId);

                // Emit Event with name of the new SKU Type
                emit NewSKUType(_shopId, skuTypeId, _name);

                // Return the new SKU Type ID
                return skuTypeId;
        }

}
```

SKUFactory.sol

```
pragma solidity ^0.5.12;

import "./SKUTypeFactory.sol";

/**
 * @title SKUFactory
 * @notice Defines functions and events related to
 * management of SKUs
 */
contract SKUFactory is SKUTypeFactory {

    /**
     * @notice emitted upon the creation of a SKU
     */
    event NewSKU(
        uint256 indexed shopId,
        uint256 skuId,
        string name
```

```
);

/**
 * @notice Create an SKU (Shopkeeping Unit) for a Shop
 * @dev Can only be run by shop owner
 */
function createSKU(
    uint256 _shopId,
    uint256 _skuTypeId,
    uint256 _price,
    string memory _name,
    string memory _desc,
    bool _consumable,
    bool _limited,
    uint256 _limit
)
    public whenNotPaused onlyShopOwner(_shopId)
    returns(uint256)
{
    // SKUs must have a non-zero price
    require(_price > 0);

    // Get SKU ID
    uint256 skuId = skus.length;

    // Create and store SKU Type
    skus.push(
        SKU(
            _shopId,
            skuId,
            _skuTypeId,
            _price,
            _name,
            _desc,
            _consumable,
            _limited,
            _limit
        )
    );

    // Add SKU to Shop's SKU list
    shopSKUs[_shopId].push(skuId);

    // Add SKU ID to SKU Type's SKU list
    skuTypeSKUs[_skuTypeId].push(skuId);
```

```
        // Emit Event with name of the new SKU
        emit NewSKU(_shopId, skuId, _name);

        // Return the new SKU ID
        return skuId;
    }

}
```

StockRoom.sol

```solidity
pragma solidity ^0.5.12;

import "./SKUFactory.sol";


/**
 * @title StockRoom
 * @notice Main contract for reference data side
 * of the In-game Pro Shop System
 */
contract StockRoom is SKUFactory {

    /**
     * @notice Set the address of the FiatContract contract
     */
    function setFiatContractAddress(address _address)
        external whenPaused onlySysAdmin
    {
        FiatContractInterface candidate =
        FiatContractInterface(_address);

        // Verify that we have the appropriate address
        require(candidate.updatedAt(0) >= 0);

        // Set the new contract address
        fiatContract = candidate;
    }

    /**
     * @notice confirm this is a StockRoom contract
     */
    function isStockRoom() external pure returns (bool) {
```

```
    return true;
}

/**
 * @notice get an item's price in Ether
 */
function getPriceInEther(uint256 _skuId)
    external view
    returns (uint256) {
    SKU memory sku = skus[_skuId];
    uint256 quote = getQuote(shops[sku.shopId].fiat);
    return quote * sku.price;
}

/**
 * @notice convert an Ether amount to the
 * Shop's fiat currency
 */
function convertEtherToShopFiat(
    uint256 _shopId,
    uint256 _amount
)
    external view
    returns (uint256) {
    uint256 quote = getQuote(shops[_shopId].fiat);
    return _amount.div(quote);
}

/**
 * @notice convert an Ether amount to the
 * Franchise's fiat currency
 */
function convertEtherToFranchiseFiat(uint256 _amount)
    external view
    returns (uint256) {
    uint256 quote = getQuote("USD");
    return _amount.div(quote);
}

/**
 * @notice get a quote for Ether in the
 * given fiat currency
 */
function getQuote(string memory _fiat)
    private view
```

```solidity
    returns (uint256) {
    bytes32 fiat = keccak256(abi.encodePacked(_fiat));
    uint256 quote;
    if (fiat == keccak256("USD")) {
        quote = fiatContract.USD(0);
    } else if (fiat == keccak256("EUR")) {
        quote = fiatContract.EUR(0);
    } else if (fiat == keccak256("GBP")) {
        quote = fiatContract.GBP(0);
    } else {
        quote = fiatContract.USD(0); // franchise
    }
    return quote;
}

/**
 * @notice confirm whether an item can be minted
 * based on limit and current item count
 */
function canMintItem(
    uint256 _skuId,
    uint256
    _itemCount
)
    external view
    returns (bool) {
    return (
        !skus[_skuId].limited ||
        (_itemCount < skus[_skuId].limit)
    );
}

/**
 * @notice Get the list of SKU Ids associated
 * with a given SKUType
 */
function getSKUTypeSKUIds(
    uint256 _skuTypeId
)
    external view
    returns (uint[] memory) {
    return skuTypeSKUs[_skuTypeId];
}

/**
```

```
 * @notice Get the list of SKU Ids
 * associated with a given Shop
 */
function getSKUIds(
    uint256 _shopId
)
    external view
    returns (uint[] memory) {
    return shopSKUs[_shopId];
}

/**
 * @notice Get a SKU's properties by ID
 */
function getSKU(
    uint256 _skuId
)
    external view
    returns (
        uint256,
        uint256,
        uint256,
        uint256,
        string memory,
        string memory,
        bool,
        bool,
        uint256
) {
    require(_skuId < skus.length);
    SKU memory sku = skus[_skuId];
    return (
        sku.shopId,
        sku.skuId,
        sku.skuTypeId,
        sku.price,
        sku.name,
        sku.description,
        sku.consumable,
        sku.limited,
        sku.limit
    );
}

/**
```

```solidity
 * @notice Get the list of SKU Type Ids
 * associated with a given Shop
 */
function getSKUTypeIds(
    uint256 _shopId
)
    external view
    returns (uint[] memory) {
    return shopSKUTypes[_shopId];
}


/**
 * @notice Get a SKUTypes properties by ID
 */
function getSKUType(
    uint256 _skuTypeId
)
    external view
    returns (
        uint256,
        uint256,
        string memory,
        string memory
) {
    require(_skuTypeId < skuTypes.length);
    SKUType memory skuType = skuTypes[_skuTypeId];
    return (
        skuType.shopId,
        skuType.skuTypeId,
        skuType.name,
        skuType.description
    );
}

/** @notice Get the list of Shop Ids
 * associated with a given Owner
 */
function getShopIds(address _owner)
    external view
    returns (uint[] memory) {
    return ownedShops[_owner];
}

// @notice Get a Shop's properties by ID
function getShop(uint256 _shopId)
```

```
        external view
        returns (
            address,
            uint256,
            string memory,
            string memory,
            string memory
    ) {
        require(_shopId < shops.length);
        Shop memory shop = shops[_shopId];
        return (
            shop.owner,
            shop.shopId,
            shop.name,
            shop.description,
            shop.fiat
        );
    }

    /**
     * @notice Get a Shop's owner
     */
    function getShopOwner(uint256 _shopId)
        external view
        returns (address) {
        require(_shopId < shops.length);
        return shops[_shopId].owner;
    }

}
```

StockRoomInterface.sol

```
pragma solidity ^0.5.12;


/**
 * @title StockRoomInterface
 * @notice Interface for StockRoom contract
 */
interface StockRoomInterface {

    /**
     * @notice Set the address of FiatContract
```

```
    */
function setFiatContractAddress(address _address)
    external;

/**
 * @notice Create a Shop
 */
function createShop(
    string calldata _name,
    string calldata _desc,
    string calldata _fiat
) external returns (uint256);

/**
 * @notice Create a SKU for a Shop
 */
function createSKU(
    uint256 _shopId,
    uint256 _skuTypeId,
    uint256 _price,
    string calldata _name,
    string calldata _desc,
    bool _consumable,
    bool _limited,
    uint256 _limit
) external returns(uint256);

/**
 * @notice Create a SKU Type for a Shop
 */
function createSKUType(
    uint256 _shopId,
    string calldata _name,
    string calldata _desc
) external returns(uint256);

/**
 * @notice get an SKU's price in Ether
 */
function getPriceInEther(uint256 _skuId)
    external view
    returns (uint256);

/**
 * @notice convert an Ether amount to a
```

```
 * Shop's fiat currency
 */
function convertEtherToShopFiat(
    uint256 _shopId,
    uint256 _amount
) external view returns (uint256);

/**
 * @notice convert an Ether amount to the
 * Franchise's fiat currency
 */
function convertEtherToFranchiseFiat(uint256 _amount)
    external view
    returns (uint256);

/**
 * @notice confirm this is a StockRoom contract
 */
function isStockRoom()
    external pure
    returns (bool);

/**
 * @notice confirm whether an item can be minted
 * based on limit and current item count
 */
function canMintItem(uint256 _skuId, uint256 _itemCount)
    external view
    returns (bool);

/**
 * @notice Get a SKU's properties by ID
 */
function getSKU(uint256 _skuId)
    external view
    returns (
        uint256,
        uint256,
        uint256,
        uint256,
        string memory,
        string memory,
        bool,
        bool,
        uint256
```

```
        );

/**
 * @notice Get the list of SKU Ids
 * associated with a given SKUType
 */
function getSKUTypeSKUIds(uint256 _skuTypeId)
    external view
    returns (uint[] memory);

/**
 * @notice Get the list of SKU Ids
 * associated with a given Shop
 */
function getSKUIds(uint256 _shopId)
    external view
    returns (uint[] memory);

/**
 * @notice Get the list of SKU Type Ids
 * associated with a given Shop
 */
function getSKUTypeIds(uint256 _shopId)
    external view
    returns (uint[] memory);

/**
 * @notice Get a SKUType's properties by ID
 */
function getSKUType(uint256 _skuTypeId)
    external view
    returns (
      uint256,
      uint256,
      string memory,
      string memory
    );

/**
 * @notice Get the list of Shop Ids
 * associated with a given Owner
 */
function getShopIds(address _owner)
    external view
    returns (uint[] memory);
```

```
/**
 * @notice Get a Shop's properties by ID
 */
function getShop(uint256 _shopId)
    external view
    returns (
      address,
      uint256,
      string memory,
      string memory,
      string memory
    );

/**
 * @notice Get a Shop's owner
 */
function getShopOwner(uint256 _shopId)
    external view
    returns (address);

}
```

The ProShop Lineage

The *ProShop* contract lineage is concerned with minting new Items (ERC-721 tokens), and the accounting associated with related income. This is where actual ETH is accumulated. It is where balances for the Franchise and each Shop are tracked. The lineage is much shallower than that of the *StockRoom* contract. There are only three levels; a base contract that defines data structures, mappings, and state variables, a factory that mints items, accepting ETH in payment, and a top level that allows checking and withdrawal of balances along with some lookup functions.

In addition to inheriting from *AccessControl* (and by way of it, Open Zeppelin's *Roles* and *SafeMath*), it also extends Open Zeppelin's *ERC721Full* contract. Remember, Solidity smart contracts can have multiple parents. You'll notice the interesting way that the *ProShopBase* constructor is declared. It has to pass the token name and token symbol to *ERC721Full* and does so not in the body of the constructor, but in the position of a modifier in the constructor signature.

ProShopBase.sol

```
pragma solidity ^0.5.12;

import "openzeppelin-solidity/contracts/token/ERC721/ERC721Full.-
sol";
```

```
import "./AccessControl.sol";
import "./StockRoomInterface.sol";

/**
 * @title ProShopBase
 * @notice Defines collections, mappings, and structs
 * for the sales side of the In-game Pro Shop System
 */
contract ProShopBase is ERC721Full, AccessControl {

    constructor() public ERC721Full(TOKEN_NAME, TOKEN_SYMBOL) {}
    StockRoomInterface internal stockRoom;

    /**
     * @dev modifier to scope access to owner of given shop
     */
    modifier onlyShopOwner(uint256 _shopId) {
        address owner = stockRoom.getShopOwner(_shopId);
        require(msg.sender == owner);
        _;
    }

    /**
     * @notice Name of the non fungible token
     */
    string public constant TOKEN_NAME = "InAppProShopItem";

    /**
     * @notice Symbol of the non fungible token
     */
    string public constant TOKEN_SYMBOL = "IAPS";

    /**
     * @notice All of the Items
     */
    Item[] public items;

    /**
     * @dev Mapping of SKU id to Item list
     */
    mapping (uint256 => uint256[]) public skuItems;

    /**
     * @dev Mapping of Shop ID to SKU list
     */
```

```solidity
mapping (uint256 => uint256[]) public shopItems;

/**
 * @dev Mapping of Owner Address to list of owned Items
 */
mapping (address => uint256[]) public ownedItems;

/**
 * @dev Mapping of Shop ID to its available Ether balance
 */
mapping (uint256 => uint256) public shopBalances;

/**
 * @notice The franchise owner's available balance
 */
uint256 public franchiseBalance;

/**
 * @notice The percentage of each transaction
 * taken by the franchise (between 0 and 100)
 */
uint256 public franchiseFeePercent;

/**
 * @notice Structure of a Pro Shop Item
 */
struct Item {

    // Owner of the item
    address owner;

    // The shop this item belongs to
    uint256 shopId;

    // The id of this item
    uint256 itemId;

    // Id of SKU of this item
    uint256 skuId;

    // Has the item been consumed?
    bool consumed;
}

}
```

ItemFactory.sol

```solidity
pragma solidity ^0.5.12;

import "./ProShopBase.sol";


/**
 * @title ItemFactory
 * @notice Defines factory and events related to
 * salable Items (ERC721 tokens)
 */
contract ItemFactory is ProShopBase {

    /**
     * @notice emitted upon the creation of an Item
     */
    event NewItem(
        uint256 indexed shopId,
        uint256 indexed skuId,
        uint256 itemId,
        uint256 amount,
        uint256 fee,
        uint256 net
    );

    /**
     * @notice Create an Item
     */
    function createItem(
        uint256 _shopId,
        uint256 _skuId
    )
        public payable whenNotPaused
        returns (uint256)
    {
        // Make sure the item can be minted
        require(
            stockRoom.canMintItem(
                _skuId,
                skuItems[_skuId].length
            ) == true
        );
```

```solidity
// Make sure enough Ether has been sent
require(msg.value == stockRoom.getPriceInEther(_skuId));

// Calculate and store the franchise fee
uint256 franchiseFee =
    uint256(
        msg.value
        .div(100)
        .mul(franchiseFeePercent)
    );
franchiseBalance = franchiseBalance.add(franchiseFee);

// Calculate and store the Shop's net sale amount
uint256 shopNetSale = msg.value.sub(franchiseFee);
shopBalances[_shopId] =
  shopBalances[_shopId].add(shopNetSale);

// Get the item id
uint256 itemId = items.length;

// Get the owner address
address owner = msg.sender;

// Create and store Item
items.push(Item(owner, _shopId, itemId, _skuId, false));

// Add Item ID to Owner's Items list
ownedItems[owner].push(itemId);

// Add the item to the Shop's list of Items minted
shopItems[_shopId].push(itemId);

// Add the item to the SKU's list of Items minted
skuItems[_skuId].push(itemId);

// Mint the token
super._mint(owner, itemId);

// Emit event with the name of the new Item
emit NewItem(
    _shopId,
    _skuId,
    itemId,
    msg.value,
```

```
            franchiseFee,
            shopNetSale
        );

        // Return the new Item ID
        return itemId;
    }

}
```

ProShop.sol

```solidity
pragma solidity ^0.5.12;

import "./ItemFactory.sol";


/**
 * @title ProShop
 * @notice Main contract for sales side
 * of the In-game Pro Shop System
 */
contract ProShop is ItemFactory {

    /**
     * @notice emitted upon the withdrawal
     * of a Shop's balance
     */
    event ShopBalanceWithdrawn(
        uint256 indexed shopId,
        uint256 amount
    );

    /**
     * @notice emitted upon the withdrawal
     * of the franchise's balance
     */
    event FranchiseBalanceWithdrawn(uint256 amount);

    constructor() public {
        // Set percentage of each sale going
        // to the franchise owner
        franchiseFeePercent = 3;
    }
```

```solidity
/**
 * @notice Set the address of the StockRoom contract
 */
function setStockRoomContractAddress(address _address)
    external onlySysAdmin
{
    StockRoomInterface candidate =
      StockRoomInterface(_address);

    // Verify that we have the appropriate address
    require(candidate.isStockRoom());

    // Set the new contract address
    stockRoom = candidate;
}

/**
 * @notice Allow a shop owner to withdraw
 * the accumulated balance of their shop, if any
 */
function withdrawShopBalance(uint256 _shopId)
    external whenNotPaused
    onlyShopOwner(_shopId)
{
    uint256 amount = shopBalances[_shopId];
    require(amount > 0 && address(this).balance >= amount);
    shopBalances[_shopId] = 0;
    msg.sender.transfer(amount);
    emit ShopBalanceWithdrawn(_shopId, amount);
}

/**
 * @notice Allow the franchise owner to withdraw
 * their accumulated balance, if any
 */
function withdrawFranchiseBalance()
    external whenNotPaused
    onlyFranchiseOwner
{
    uint256 amount = franchiseBalance;
    require(amount > 0 && address(this).balance >= amount);
    franchiseBalance = 0;
    msg.sender.transfer(amount);
    emit FranchiseBalanceWithdrawn(amount);
```

```
    }

    /**
     * @notice Allow a shop owner to check the
     * accumulated balance of their shop in Ether or Shop fiat
     */
    function checkShopBalance(uint256 _shopId, bool _inFiat)
        external view onlyShopOwner(_shopId)
        returns(uint256)
    {
        uint256 balance = shopBalances[_shopId];
        return (balance > 0 && _inFiat)
          ? stockRoom.convertEtherToShopFiat(_shopId, balance)
          : balance;
    }

    /**
     * @notice Allow the franchise owner to check their
     * accumulated balance in Ether or franchise fiat
     */
    function checkFranchiseBalance(bool _inFiat)
        external view onlyFranchiseOwner()
        returns(uint256)
    {
        return (franchiseBalance > 0 && _inFiat)
          ? stockRoom
            .convertEtherToFranchiseFiat(franchiseBalance)
          : franchiseBalance;
    }

    /**
     * @notice Get the list of Item Ids
     * associated with a given Owner
    function getItemIds(address _owner)
        external view
        returns (uint[] memory)
    {
        return ownedItems[_owner];
    }

    /**
     * @notice Get the count of minted Items
     * associated with a given Shop
     */
    function getShopItemCount(uint256 _shopId)
```

```solidity
    external view
    returns (uint256)
{
    return shopItems[_shopId].length;
}

/**
 * @notice Get the count of minted Items
 * associated with a given SKU
 */
function getSKUItemCount(uint256 _skuId)
    external view
    returns (uint256)
{
    return skuItems[_skuId].length;
}

/**
 * @notice Get the count of Items associated
 * with a given Owner
 */
function getOwnerItemCount(address _owner)
    external view
    returns (uint256)
{
    return ownedItems[_owner].length;
}

}
```

The FiatContract Interface

Our contract gets quotes for ETH in several fiat currencies (USD, GBP, and EUR) from a third party contract called *FiatContract*. As described earlier, in the section on oracles, that contract is updated hourly by an external mechanism. Gas for the update transactions is paid for with ETH from an address which accepts donations. Thus if you depend upon its operation, you can donate ETH to that address to keep it going.

We deploy a copy of *FiatContract* locally and initialize it with some relatively sane values programmatically as part of the contract migration process. This allows us to test our interaction with it. In order to understand how to talk to that contract, we include *FiatContractInterface* in *StockRoomBase*.

In the *StockRoom* contract, we have a function `setFiatContractAddress` which accepts the address for the *FiatContract* instance to talk to. It casts the address to the *FiatContractInterface* type in order to invoke a function on it.

```
/**
 * @notice Set the address of the FiatContract contract
 */
function setFiatContractAddress(address _address)
    external
    whenPaused
    onlySysAdmin
{
    FiatContractInterface candidate =
```

```
FiatContractInterface(_address);

    // Verify that we have the appropriate address
    require(candidate.updatedAt(0) >= 0);

    // Set the new contract address
    fiatContract = candidate;
}
```

Unfortunately, *FiatContract* provides no intentional way for a calling contract to be certain that the address it has been given is actually the address of a *FiatContract* instance. So what we do is to make certain that a call to **updatedAt(0)** returns a value greater than or equal to zero. If this fails, we know the address is incorrect and the transaction fails.

Although we do deploy a version of *FiatContract* for testing, its implementation is unimportant to us; only the interface we use to communicate with it is salient. It will be included in this chapter since it is compiled into our *StockRoom* contract and would required even on the mainnet, in order to talk to the actual *FiatContract* instance deployed there.

FiatContractInterfacel.sol

```
pragma solidity ^0.5.12;


/**
 * @title FiatContractInterface
 * @notice Interface for third-party contract
 * FiatContract (see: https://fiatcontract.com/)
 */
interface  FiatContractInterface {

    function ETH(uint _id) external view returns (uint256);

    function USD(uint _id) external view returns (uint256);
```

```
    function EUR(uint _id) external view returns (uint256);

    function GBP(uint _id) external view returns (uint256);

    function updatedAt(uint _id) external view returns (uint);
}
```

Summary

This chapter covered a lot of important ground for those new to Solidity.

Here are a few important things to remember:
- The block gas limit puts a hard ceiling on the size of your contracts, so keep them as small as possible, implementing functionality only when it's needed, and not speculatively.
- Every separately deployed contract in your system increases its attack surface, so keep it all in one contract if you can.
- Use inheritance to stratify the functionality of your contract. Each subclass (sub-contract?) should be ordered such that any internal functionality it requires exists in one of its superclasses (super-contracts?).
- The compiled byte code of the final contract at the tip of an inheritance chain contains all the inherited code, and can be deployed by itself.
- Smart contracts often deal with actual currency, so be careful. Keep abreast of the known vulnerabilities, and follow the patterns and best practices adopted by the community.
- The Open Zeppelin project offers a great set of contracts to help you implement common patterns safely, so familiarize

yourself with their offerings before rebuilding the wheel in a potentially more vulnerable way.

- Oracles are a way to update contracts with data from the off-blockchain world. Since they typically write data to the contract, the transactions they send cost real money. Operation of an oracle therefore requires a funding source and a strategy to keep those funds topped up.

CHAPTER FIVE

Testing Contracts

Regardless of the programming language we use, unit testing helps us to maintain confidence in our ongoing development efforts as we add new and refactor existing functionality. But often, owing to deadlines, dislike of "grunt work", or just general laziness, we skip unit tests. "The proof is in the pudding," some say. "If the new feature works and doesn't seem to have broken any of the old ones, why waste time writing unit tests?"

Personally, I could debate either side of that age-old holy war with gusto. I like to seek a happy medium of testing the truly important bits without sweating 100% coverage just for the sake of ticking all the boxes. If a client is footing the bill, it's up to them to set priorities and I happily follow suit. But with Solidity and Ethereum, perhaps more so than with any other programming paradigm, I can unequivocally state that unit tests are *absolutely necessary*.

Determining what went wrong with a reverted transaction is difficult. While Truffle allows you to debug transactions, the process is tedious at best. Inspecting the state of a deployed contract isn't as simple an undertaking as with most database platforms. Plus, the language is evolving rapidly enough that you may have to endure multiple deprecations during the course of a six-month project. Ensuring that your code continues to work throughout all this is impossible without including your unit tests in the critical path.

In short, without unit testing, you won't get far with Solidity development. Write the essential parts of your contracts, test them, and then move on to building the UI that interacts with them.

Code Under Test

Thus far, we've looked at some examples of contract code from the In-App Pro Shop project, focusing mainly on inheritance, functions, modifiers, and events. We've also reviewed source code for the full suite of contracts, to get a sense of scope for the entire system.

In order to frame the subject of smart contract unit testing, we need to focus a little more on data structures and pick one of our contracts to test.

The very first use case once a user has connected their account to the application is that they should be able to create a Shop. Until that happens, there's really nothing else for them to do. So let's examine the parts of the contract code that support that and the unit tests that ensure it works.

Shop Data

In this excerpt from *StockRoomBase.sol*, we see the data structure and and a few of the contract state variables associated with maintenance of Shops.

```
// StockroomBase.sol - partial code below...
contract StockRoomBase is AccessControl {

    Shop[] public shops;

    mapping (uint256 => address) public shopToOwner;
    mapping (address => uint256[]) public ownedShops;

    struct Shop {

        // Owner of the item
        address owner;

        // The id of this shop
        uint256 shopId;

        // Name of the item
        string name;

        // Description of the shop
        string description;

        // Fiat currency for prices
        string fiat;
    }
}
```

The Shops Array

First, we have a `public array` called `shops` whose members will be of type `Shop`. This will hold all the Shops created by users of the system. As in Javascript and other languages, the `[ ]` is what indicates the variable is of the `array` type. That's a pretty straightforward and unsurprising declaration of a typed collection.

```
Shop[] public shops;
```

Mappings

Next, we have a couple of `mapping` declarations called `shopToOwner` and `ownedShops`. In Solidity, mappings are basically key/value pairs, with specific types for key and value.

In the case of `shopToOwner`, we have keys of type `uint256` and values of type `address`. Our Shop identifiers are going to be unsigned 256-bit integers, and owners are identified in the system by an Ethereum address. So when we need to determine the owner of a Shop for which we have an ID, this mapping enables a quick lookup.

In the `ownedShops` mapping, we have an `address` for a key and an `array` of `uint256` numbers as the value. Since a Shop Owner may have any number of Shops in this system, this mapping is maintained to give us a quick list of all the Shop IDs for a given Shop Owner's Ethereum address.

```
mapping (uint256 => address) public shopToOwner;

mapping (address => uint256[]) public ownedShops;
```

The Shop Struct

Finally, we see a `struct` called `Shop`. This is a custom data type that defines the structure of a Shop entity within our system. We have the expected Shop Owner `address` and `shopId`, then three `string` values for `name`, `description`, and `fiat`. Of these, the last is the only one that needs any explanation.

Prices need to be set in a stable fiat currency, like USD, so the Shop Owner doesn't have to change them every time the value of Ether skyrockets or nosedives. Accordingly, we need the Shop Owner to specify a fiat currency for the Shop, and all prices will be expressed in that currency, to be converted to Ether at the time of a purchase.

```
struct Shop {

    // Owner of the item
    address owner;

    // The id of this shop
    uint256 shopId;

    // Name of the item
    string name;

    // Description of the shop
    string description;

    // Fiat currency for prices
    string fiat;
}
```

Shop Factory

The factory function that allows us to create `Shop` instances is defined in the *ShopFactory* contract, and defines the `event` that will be emitted when one is created.

```
// ShopFactory.sol

contract ShopFactory is StockRoomBase {

    event NewShop(
        address indexed owner,
        uint256 shopId,
        string name
                        );

    function createShop(
        string _name,
        string _desc,
        string _fiat
    )
        external
        whenNotPaused
        returns (uint256)
    {
        // Get Shop ID and owner address
        uint256 shopId = shops.length;
        address owner = msg.sender;

        // Create and store Shop
        shops.push(Shop(owner, shopId, _name, _desc, _fiat));

        // Map Shop ID to owner address
```

```
        shopToOwner[shopId] = owner;

        // Add Shop ID to Owner's Shops list
        ownedShops[owner].push(shopId);

        // Give the owner the ROLE_SHOP_OWNER role
        addRole(owner, ROLE_SHOP_OWNER);

        // Send an event with the name of the new shop
        emit NewShop(owner, shopId, _name);

        // Return the new Shop ID
        return shopId;
    }
}
```

The Event

Let's look at the event first. It's called NewShop and takes three arguments; owner, shopId, and name. These are all data from the Shop structure, and their types are stated here. The one unique thing to take notice of is the keyword indexed preceding owner. What's that about?

When a client application listens for events of a certain type from the EVM, they may not want to receive all such events. For instance, if the Shop Owner is using the Shop maintenance application, they don't need to be notified of every Shop instance that's created, only those that *they* create. Solidity's indexed keyword allows us to filter events based on that field.

```
event NewShop(address indexed owner, uint256 shopId, string name);
```

The Factory Function

Next, the createShop factory function. It takes the three string properties of the Shop struct as arguments; name, description, and `fiat`. Its modifiers ensure it can only be called externally (not from other functions in this contract), when the contract is not paused. It will return a 256-bit unsigned integer representing the Shop ID.

The first thing it does is define the new Shop's ID to be the length of the `shops` array. Initially, I thought this should be a UUID-like identifier, based on a mix of the timestamp and a random number or some such. This led to the discovery that creating a random number in Solidity is not a simple endeavor.

The simplest thing to do is to use the length of the array for the ID, and if an item is deleted, you just (optionally) clear the data at the deleted location, remove any pointers to it and move on. Access to the data in the array is by mapping anyway, so there's never really a need to traverse the entire array, and items not in the mapping are for all intents and purposes unreachable.

To be clear, the ID of the Shop is synonymous with its array index. This requires that we not reorganize the array on delete, but that's fine, because it saves gas.

After getting the new Shop's ID, we store the `msg.sender` address in a variable called `owner`. Then we create a new `Shop` structure and push it onto the `shops` array.

Now, we need to update the mappings. First, the Shop Owner's address is mapped to the Shop ID in `shopToOwner`. Then we push the Shop ID onto the Shop Owner's array in `ownedShops`. Note that we haven't had to check that the array was initialized if this is the first Shop for this owner. Nice, right? It just exists when we try to access it.

After updating the mappings, we add the Shop Owner role to the `owner` address. This has no effect if the Shop Owner already has the role, but it's important that it happen on the first creation. No need to spend extra gas checking for the role before adding it.

Finally, we emit a `NewShop` event, passing the `owner`, `shopId`, and `name`.

```
function createShop(
    string calldata _name,
    string calldata _desc,
    string calldata _fiat
)
    external
    whenNotPaused
    returns (uint256)
{
    // Get Shop ID and owner address
    uint256 shopId = shops.length;
    address owner = msg.sender;

    // Create and store Shop
    shops.push(Shop(owner, shopId, _name, _desc, _fiat));

    // Map Shop ID to owner address
    shopToOwner[shopId] = owner;

    // Add Shop ID to Owner's Shops list
    ownedShops[owner].push(shopId);

    // Give the owner the ROLE_SHOP_OWNER role
    addRole(owner, ROLE_SHOP_OWNER);

    // Send an event with the name of the new shop
    emit NewShop(owner, shopId, _name);

    // Return the new Shop ID
    return shopId;
}
```

Links

Creating a Random Number in Solidity
`bit.ly/2FTLTZ0`

Shop View Functions

Now that we've seen the data structure, state variables, and factory function associated with Shop creation, we have just a couple of other Shop-related functions to review. Those are view functions, which simply fetch data from the blockchain. These were moved out of *ShopFactory.sol* and into *StockRoom.sol* during the massive refactor that occurred after the great bifurcation event.

```
// StockRoom.sol - Partial code below...

contract StockRoom is SKUFactory {

    function getShopIds(address _owner)
        external
        view
        returns (uint[] memory)
    {
        return ownedShops[_owner];
    }

    function getShop(uint256 _shopId)
        external
        view
        returns (address, uint256, string, string, string)
    {
        require(_shopId < shops.length);
        Shop memory shop = shops[_shopId];
        return (
            shop.owner,
            shop.shopId,
            shop.name,
```

```
        shop.description,
        shop.fiat
    );
  }

}
```

The getShopIds Function

The `getShopIds` function expects a Shop Owner's `address` as its single argument, and it can only be called externally. Marked as `view`, it can retrieve data but not write it, and can only call other `view` or `pure` functions.

Tangentially related, the `pure` function modifier means the function has mostly the same limitations as `view`, but is more restrictive in that it can't read data and can only call other "pure" functions.

Also note that this function returns a `uint` array marked `memory`. Yikes, what's this about?

First, if you were paying attention earlier, you know our `owned-Shops` mapping maps the Shop Owner's `address` to a `uint256` array. Why would we be returning a `uint` array here? Just because `uint` is an alias for `uint256`, and can be used interchangeably.

But that's probably not what threw you. What's that `memory` modifier? Complex types (i.e., arrays and structs) need to have a so-called data location annotation when specified as function arguments or return types. This helps the EVM manage whether copies of data are made in calls between functions.

```
    function getShopIds(address _owner)
        external
        view
        returns (uint[] memory)
    {
        return ownedShops[_owner];
```

```
}
```

The getShop Function

Moving on, we have a more interesting function in `getShop`. It's also marked `external` and `view`, but the return type is unexpectedly weird. Instead of the `Shop` struct you might think we'd be returning, we actually list five data types.

Currently, Solidity isn't capable of returning a struct type, but it *can* return multiple values. So what this function does is get the `Shop` instance with the given `shopId` and return all its properties at once. Solidity `0.6.0` will allow returning a `struct`, making this much easier.

```
function getShop(uint256 _shopId)
    external view
    returns (
      address, uint256,
      string, string memory,
      string memory
                      ) {
    require(_shopId < shops.length);
    Shop memory shop = shops[_shopId];
    return (
        shop.owner,
        shop.shopId,
        shop.name,
        shop.description,
        shop.fiat
    );
}
```

Links

Solidity Data Location Documentation
`bit.ly/2JfV3zC`

Solidity Testing with Truffle

Unit testing Solidity contracts, when using Truffle, can be achieved with JavaScript, TypeScript, or Solidity.

We're going to use the JavaScript approach, which is done with the Mocha testing framework and Chai for assertions. These are built into the Truffle framework, so there's no need to install them separately, but it's good to be familiar with how they work, so if you haven't used them before you might want to nip off and have a look at their websites in the Links section first.

Links

Mocha
`mochajs.org`

Chai
`chaijs.com`

Shop Factory Tests

If you need a refresher on where in the project structure unit tests for the contracts go and how to run them from Truffle console, refer back to the chapter on setting up the local environment. At this point, we'll just jump right into the *ShopFactoryTest.js* file and see what's going on there.

```
// ShopFactoryTest.js - partial code below...

const StockRoom = artifacts.require("./StockRoom.sol");

contract('ShopFactory', function(accounts) {

    let contract ;
    const shopOwner = accounts[1];

    before(async () => {
        // Get the contract instance for this suite
        contract  = await StockRoom.new();

        // Unpause the contract
        await contract.unpause();

    });

    it("should allow anyone to create a shop", async function()
{ ... });

    it("should allow a shop owner to create another shop", async
function() { ... });
```

```
    it("should allow a shop owner retrieve a list of their shops",
async function() { ... });

    it("should allow shop owner retrieve a shop by id", async
function() { ... });

});
```

In this overview, the bodies of the individual tests are collapsed, so we can review the structure of the test file. You'll notice a few differences from ordinary JavaScript Mocha tests, namely the use of `contract` instead of `describe` for setting up the suite, and of `artifacts.require` for importing the Solidity source code.

The "Cleanroom Environment"

One thing to know about the way these tests work is that Truffle will ensure the tests in each file don't interfere with each other via snapshotting or redeployment of your contracts (depending upon the Ethereum client you're using). This happens between execution of each test file, not before each test within a file. If you don't want that, you can place each test by itself in its own file.

Usually, with unit testing, we don't want one test to depend upon the outcome of previous tests. But for things like making sure that the Shop Owner can create another Shop after creating their first one, and that the Shop ID assigned to that second Shop is the next index number in the `shops` array, it is sort of handy that Solidity testing works this way by default. It's just important to understand it going in.

Instantiating the Contract

First, we get a manipulatable instance of the *ShopFactory* contract into by way of the `artifacts.require` statement. This uses Truffle's contract abstraction to represent the contract in JavaScript so that we can manipulate it easily.

```
const StockRoom = artifacts.require("./StockRoom.sol");
```

Creating the Test Wrapper

We use the `contract` function to declare our test set. Here, we're passing it the name of our test set "ShopFactory" and the function containing our test set which will expect an array of the account addresses that are available. Truffle will inject the accounts it retrieves from its connection to Ganache.

```
contract('ShopFactory', function(accounts) { ... });
```

Accessing Accounts

You may remember from a previous installment that Ganache generates ten accounts, and we've set it up to generate the same ten accounts every time it starts. This means we can hardcode the actual account addresses if we want, but to be safe, we can just refer to the addresses by their array indices. In this test, we've said the Shop Owner will be the address at index 1.

```
let contract ;
const shopOwner = accounts[1];
```

Pre-test Setup

The `before` function performs any setup necessary prior to executing all the tests. We're going to use `async`/`await` to simplify the process of instantiating the contract and then un-pausing it. Recall that when our contracts are constructed they are paused. They're un-paused by the migration script once everything is deployed. Inside the test, however, the migration script isn't run. We're using Truffle's contract abstraction, so we have to unpause the script here before we can use it.

```
before(async () => {
    // Get the contract instance for this suite
    contract  = await StockRoom.new();

    // Unpause the contract
    await contract.unpause();

});
```

Now let's have a look at the first test, which confirms that *Shop-Factory* should allow anyone to create a Shop.

Testing the Shop Factory

We know that the `createShop` function on the ShopFactory contract requires `name`, `description`, and `fiat` as arguments. We define those in the constants `shopName`, `shopDesc`, and `shopFiat`.

We know that the `shopId` should be 0 because the contract is brand new, and this is the first `Shop` created. We will wrap that number in a `BN` instance, which represents big numbers, larger than Javascript can safely handle on its own.

Also, notice that we invoke the function with an additional argument; an object with a `from` property set to the Shop Owner's address, shopOwner. When the Solidity function is invoked, the `msg.sender` will be set to this address.

Next we assert that the appropriate event was emitted and that it had the values we expect. Note that the shopId is a `BN` instance (because currently the *web3.js* library uses *BN.js* to represent big numbers). We use its `eq` function to check its equality against the `shopId` we expect (and wrapped in a `BN` instance earlier).

Once our event listener is in place, we actually invoke the `createShop` function for real by passing it the arguments rather than chaining to `call`. We use `await` to hold up the thread of execution until the transaction is complete, then we go ahead and fetch the Shop IDs for the Shop Owner invoking the `getShopIds` contract function, and assert that its length is 1.

```
it("should allow anyone to create a shop", async function() {

  // The name and description of the new shop
  const shopName = "Barely Legal Pawn";
  const shopDesc = "Great stuff, cheap!";
  const shopFiat = "USD";
  const shopId = new BN(0, 10);

  // Now call the function and write the data
  const result = await contract.createShop(
  shopName, shopDesc, shopFiat, {from: shopOwner});

  // Test that appropriate event was emitted
  truffleAssert.eventEmitted(result, 'NewShop', (event) => {
      return (
        event.owner === shopOwner &&
        event.name === shopName &&
        event.shopId.eq(shopId)
      );
  }, 'NewShop event should be emitted with correct info');

  // Make sure the shop count for this owner is correct
```

```
const shopIds = await contract.getShopIds(shopOwner);
assert.equal(shopIds.length, 1, "Shop count wasn't correct");

});
```

That's the first test in this set. The next two are very similar. Lets have a look at the last test, which fetches a Shop.

Testing the getShop Function

Here we're going to retrieve the Shop we created in the first test. We know what the values should be, we just need to test that they're returned properly when we invoke the `getShop` contract function. Remember, that since we couldn't return a structure, we had to return the individual properties. Unsurprisingly, that shows up as an array. We just have to make assertions against each of its elements.

The only really notable part of this test, then, is that when comparing the second element to the `shopId` constant, we use `shop[1].eq(shopId)`. That's because the Shop ID is a `uint256`, which is represented on the JavaScript side as a `BN` instance. It won't automatically be cast to `Number` in an expression, and even though we could, we don't want to convert it to a JavaScript number, because a `uint256` value can easily exceed `Number.-MAX_SAFE_INTEGER`. Therefore we use BN's `eq()` method to perform comparisons.

```
it("should allow shop owner retrieve a shop by id", async
function() {

    // The name and description of the new shop
    const shopName = "Barely Legal Pawn";
    const shopDesc = "Great stuff, cheap!";
```

```
const shopFiat = "USD";
const shopId = new BN(0, 10);

// Make sure the owner's Shop count is correct
const shop = await contract.getShop(shopId);

assert.equal(shop[0], shopOwner, "Shop owner address wrong");
assert.equal(shop[1].eq(shopId), "Shop ID wrong");
assert.equal(shop[2], shopName,  "Shop name wrong");
assert.equal(shop[3], shopDesc,  "Shop description wrong");
assert.equal(shop[4], shopFiat,  "Shop fiat currency wrong");

});
```

Links

BN.js
bit.ly/2Nm6KYF

Running Specific Tests

With Ganache already running, from the Truffle Console, we can just type `test` to run all the tests it can find, or we can specify just which tests we want to run. In this case, we'll just run the tests in *ShopFactoryTest.js*.

```
truffle(development)> test test/ShopFactoryTest.js
truffle(development)> Using network 'development'.

Setting FiatContact address
Setting StockRoom Contract address


  Contract: ShopFactory
    ✓ should allow anyone to create a shop (424ms)
    ✓ should allow an existing shop owner to create another shop
(887ms)
    ✓ should allow shop owner retrieve a list of their shops
(73ms)
    ✓ should allow shop owner retrieve a shop by id (202ms)


  4 passing (2s)
```

Summary

Even though unit testing might not be anybody's favorite pastime, it's definitely a necessary evil when it comes to Solidity. The bright spot is it gets us up close and personal with our contracts. We can be certain they're working and learn all about interacting with them at the same time, well before we start building our application. That means it should be smooth sailing once we start engineering our UI.

CHAPTER SIX

Bootstrapping the Client

In this chapter, we'll look into the unique aspects of a client that talks to the blockchain on behalf of a user that is able to authenticate with a blockchain-aware browser. To follow along on your own system, Ganache should be running, with our contracts deployed and tested. The mock data should already be created. I'll assume you're running the MetaMask browser plugin, and have configured it as described in the chapter on setting up your local environment.

The client for this project is written in JavaScript with an architecture of React and Redux. It's beyond the scope of this book to bring you up to speed on that ecosystem, so I'm going to take it as a given that you understand or are at least passingly familiar with it.

How To Authenticate and Connect

There are two things that need to be taken care of before anything useful can happen in this client:

- Authenticate the user in some fashion so that we can make blockchain transactions on their behalf
- Connect to the blockchain so that we can send transactions or invoke functions that request data

Consequently, our first job is to understand how we will achieve those tasks.

Web3 – Low-level Ethereum API

From the application's perspective, both of the above tasks will be handled by a library called *web3.js*.

Your app's awareness of the user will be strictly reduced to list of the accounts that are made available to you by *web3.js*. All interactions with the blockchain will happen through it. You can instantiate it yourself, or you can snag MetaMask's instance. If MetaMask isn't running in your browser, then your instance can still connect to Ganache and get the accounts it created at startup.

If you visit the *web3.js* docs in the Links section below, it might seem a little daunting. It's definitely a low-level API. To use it effectively, you need to know a lot about the nitty gritty details of Ethereum. When I began the In-App Pro Shop client, I started with *web3.js* and nothing else. I was able to make progress, but I quickly realized there were a lot of places I could drop the ball.

Fortunately, our friends over at Consensys realized this and provided us with a much friendlier tool called Drizzle. If you're using React as we are, Drizzle, is just about the quickest way to get to the joy.

Drizzle – High-level Abstraction

Drizzle is based on a Redux store, which you're free to use for managing the entire state of your app. I preferred to keep application state in my own store while allowing Drizzle to maintain its own state. You are free to use Drizzle's store to maintain your own state. Or, if you're not using Redux, manage your application's state in whatever way you see fit.

You can treat Drizzle as a black box that provides you with:

- The accounts you are authorized to use
- A local cache of relevant blockchain data for speed
- Representations of your contracts, which you can use to invoke functions, listen for events, etc.

Links

Web3 Library Docs
`bit.ly/2LBgii9`

Consensys
`bit.ly/2Xr0tNi`

Drizzle
`bit.ly/2RU5ahs`

Starting Up

At startup, we need to create Drizzle's store, configured with everything it needs to know, including references to our compiled contracts. Drizzle uses React's Context API to provide us with a handle to everything we need to interact with it. In my opinion, this wasn't the best choice, but it works. It just led to an unavoidably obtuse bit of bootstrapping code which we'll see and unravel in a moment.

We also want to create our own Redux store in the usual way. Finally, we need to create our main App component. I haven't added routing to this application, primarily because to support bookmarking of a route would be overly complicated given the possibility of multiple Shop Owner accounts with multiple Shops. Bearing all this in mind, let's have a quick look at the *index.js* file for our React app.

index.js

```
// index.js - render the main application component

import React from 'react';
import ReactDOM from 'react-dom';
import { Provider } from 'react-redux';
import { DrizzleContext } from 'drizzle-react';
import { Drizzle, generateStore } from "drizzle";
```

```
import 'bootstrap/dist/css/bootstrap.css';
import 'bootstrap/dist/css/bootstrap-theme.css';

import ProShop from './abi/ProShop.json';
import StockRoom from './abi/StockRoom.json';
import App from './components/App'
import store from './store';

const drizzleOptions = {
    contracts: [
        ProShop,
        StockRoom
    ],
    events: {
        ProShop: [
            'NewItem',
            'ShopBalanceWithdrawn',
            'FranchiseBalanceWithdrawn'
        ],
        StockRoom: [
            'NewShop',
            'NewSKUType',
            'NewSKU'
        ]
    },
    web3:{
        fallback: {
            type: 'ws',
            url: 'wss://127.0.0.1:7545'
        }
    }
};

const drizzleStore = generateStore(drizzleOptions);
const drizzle = new Drizzle(drizzleOptions, drizzleStore);

function render() {
    ReactDOM.render(
        <DrizzleContext.Provider drizzle={drizzle}>
            <Provider store={store}>
                <DrizzleContext.Consumer>
                    {drizzleContext => {
                        return  <App
                            drizzleContext={drizzleContext}/>
                    }}
```

```
      </DrizzleContext.Consumer>
    </Provider>
  </DrizzleContext.Provider>,
  document.getElementById('app')
  )
}

render();
```

Imports

In the imports section, the one notable thing to touch on is the `ProShop` and `StockRoom` imports that come from the `/abi` folder. You may recall from previous chapters that we're using the *create-react-app* scripts and one of the prohibitions we're laboring under is that all imported files need to come from the `/src` folder. From React's standpoint, `/abi` is actually `/src/abi`. Also, we had to configure Truffle to output its compiled contracts to this folder so that we could import them. That was done in *truffle.js*.

```
import ReactDOM from 'react-dom';
import { Provider } from 'react-redux';
import { DrizzleContext } from 'drizzle-react';
import { Drizzle, generateStore } from "drizzle";

import 'bootstrap/dist/css/bootstrap.css';
import 'bootstrap/dist/css/bootstrap-theme.css';

import ProShop from './abi/ProShop.json';
import StockRoom from './abi/StockRoom.json';
import App from './components/App'
import store from './store';
```

Drizzle Options

First, we pass the `ProShop` and `StockRoom` imports to Drizzle in the `contracts` section. Simple enough. Drizzle will use these compiled contracts to give us our contract abstraction that we can call functions on later.

The `events` section enumerates each contract and its events which we presumably want to listen for and be notified about. As I mentioned above, this part of Drizzle is not fully implemented at the moment, so they're just here for form. Later we'll get into how we handle the events using the underlying *web3.js* library when needed.

Finally, there is a `web3` section where a fallback is defined as a websocket to a port on our localhost. This is used if Drizzle doesn't find a *web3.js* instance initialized by MetaMask. That allows us to talk to our local Ganache instance directly if MetaMask isn't installed.

```
const drizzleOptions = {
    contracts: [
        ProShop,
        StockRoom
    ],
    events: {
        ProShop: [
            'NewItem',
            'ShopBalanceWithdrawn',
            'FranchiseBalanceWithdrawn'
        ],
        StockRoom: [
            'NewShop',
            'NewSKUType',
            'NewSKU'
        ]
    },
    web3:{
        fallback: {
            type: 'ws',
            url: 'wss://127.0.0.1:7545'
        }
    }
};
```

Instantiating Drizzle and Its Store

Drizzle has its own store, which we first create with `generate-Store`, passing it the `drizzleOptions` we defined above. Then we instantiate Drizzle itself, passing in the `drizzleOptions` and the `drizzleStore` we just created. I think that could have been done with a single call to a static factory function on Drizzle, but I'm sure the architects at Consensys had their reasons for doing it this way.

```
const drizzleStore = generateStore(drizzleOptions);
const drizzle = new Drizzle(drizzleOptions, drizzleStore);
```

Rendering

I said that the Context API was maybe not the greatest choice for how to build this thing. That's mainly because only the App component uses it and React's Context API is really meant as a way of letting descendent components magically access a context created above it somewhere without having to explicitly pass that context through intermediate components that don't need it as props.

But here, only the `App` component needs access to the `Drizzle-Context`, and its needed in `componentDidUpdate` so we actually have to create the context then get the context from the consumer and pass it into the `App` component as a prop anyway.

Creating the context is done with the outer `DrizzleContext.Provider` wrapper, which we pass the `drizzle` instance to. Then we instantiate the `Provider` for our own Redux store in the usual way. Inside that wrapper, we have a `DrizzleContext.-Consumer` which takes the `drizzleContext` it gets from the `DrizzleContext.Provider` above it and returns an instance of our `App` component with `drizzleContext` as a prop.

Finally, since *index.js* is just a script and not a component, we must invoke its `render` function at the end.

Could this be simpler? Absolutely, I believe it could. But at least it's contained to this one bootstrap file, and now our `App` component can access the `DrizzleContext` and all its goodness inside `componentDidUpdate` which it will need to do in order to further orchestrate the startup process.

Regardless of startup elegance or lack thereof, let's move on and see how *App.js* takes this handoff and runs with it.

```
function render() {
    ReactDOM.render(
        <DrizzleContext.Provider drizzle={drizzle}>
            <Provider store={store}>
                <DrizzleContext.Consumer>
                    {drizzleContext => {
                        return  <App
                             drizzleContext={drizzleContext}/>
                    }}
                </DrizzleContext.Consumer>
            </Provider>
        </DrizzleContext.Provider>,
        document.getElementById('app')
    )
}

render();
```

Links

React Context API
`bit.ly/2Nx0WOr`

State Management in the App Component

In *App.js*, the component will orchestrate the rest of the startup process by watching Drizzle's state and our own store's state in its `componentDidUpdate` function and taking appropriate actions on certain changes.

In the partial extract below, you can see that function and the state and action dispatchers we've mapped to props for the component using `mapStateToProps` and `mapDispatchToProps`.

```
// App.js - partial code below ...

import React, {Component} from 'react';
import {connect} from 'react-redux';
import {ThemeProvider} from "styled-components";

import theme from "./theme/theme";
import ShopView from "./ShopView";
import SplashView from "./SplashView";
import NavigationBar from "./NavigationBar";
import {CONTRACTS} from "../constants";
import {getSKUs} from "../store/sku/SKUActions";
import {getSKUTypes} from "../store/sku_type/SKUTypeActions";
import {getShopBalance, getShops} from "../store/shop/
ShopActions";
import {accountsFetched, selectAccount} from "../store/account/
AccountActions";

import {KitWrapper} from "./theme";

class App extends Component {
```

```
componentDidUpdate(prevProps) {
    const {
        accountsFetched,
        selectAccount,
        getShops,
        selectedAccount,
        selectedShopId,
        getSKUTypes,
        getSKUs,
        accounts,
        checkShopBalance
    } = this.props;

    const {drizzleState, drizzle, initialized} =
            this.props.drizzleContext;

    // Store the accounts when drizzle initializes
    if (initialized && !prevProps.drizzleContext.initialized)
{
        if (Object.keys(drizzleState.accounts).length) {
            accountsFetched(
                Object.values(drizzleState.accounts)
            );
        }
    }

    // Select the first account when the accounts are fetched
    if (accounts && accounts.length && !prevProps.accounts) {
        selectAccount(accounts[0]);
    }

    // Get Shops when account is selected
    if (selectedAccount &&
        selectedAccount !== prevProps.selectedAccount) {
        getShops(
            drizzle.contracts[CONTRACTS.STOCK_ROOM],
            selectedAccount
        );
    }

    // Get SKUs & SKUTypes when Shop is selected
    if (selectedShopId &&
        selectedShopId !== prevProps.selectedShopId) {
        checkShopBalance(
            drizzle.contracts[CONTRACTS.PRO_SHOP],
```

```
                    selectedAccount,
                    selectedShopId
                );
                getSKUTypes(
                    drizzle.contracts[CONTRACTS.STOCK_ROOM],
                    selectedShopId
                );
                getSKUs(
                    drizzle.contracts[CONTRACTS.STOCK_ROOM],
                    selectedShopId
                );
            }

        }
}

const mapStateToProps = (state) => ({
    accounts: state.accountState.accounts,
    selectedAccount: state.accountState.selectedAccount,
    selectedShopId: state.shopState.selectedShopId,
    theme: theme.appTheme
});

const mapDispatchToProps = (dispatch) => ({
    accountsFetched: accounts =>
                dispatch(accountsFetched(accounts)),
    selectAccount: account =>
                dispatch(selectAccount(account)),
    getShops: (contract, account) =>
                dispatch(getShops(contract, account)),
    getSKUs: (contract, shopId) =>
                dispatch(getSKUs(contract, shopId)),
    getSKUTypes: (contract, shopId) =>
                dispatch(getSKUTypes(contract, shopId)),
    checkShopBalance: (contract, owner, shopId) =>
                dispatch(getShopBalance(contract, owner, shopId))

});

export default connect(mapStateToProps, mapDispatchToProps)(App);
```

From the `drizzleContext` object, we get `drizzle`, `drizzle-State`, and `initialized`. The `initialized` variable tells us when

Drizzle has managed to connect to *web3.js* and has our contracts and accounts ready to work with.

We're going to take our actions in `componentDidUpdate` only when something changes, and we know that by comparing the current values to the previous props. This is important so that we don't get into a loop of continuously performing an action.

This function handles not only the startup of the app, but also a few state changes that are necessary when the user changes the selected account or Shop.

Things That Happen Automatically at Startup

- Store the accounts when Drizzle initializes
- Select the first account when the accounts are fetched
- Get Shops when an account is selected

If you are connecting to Ganache, you might get ten accounts when Drizzle initializes. If you're connecting to MetaMask, you'll only get its selected account. The former case is most likely true only during development and testing. If almost all of the time we're only going to get a single account to work with, then we don't want the user to have to manually open the Accounts menu and select their sole account. So, we'll automatically select it.

Further, when whenever an account is selected (automatically at startup or later by the user), we'll want to fetch all the Shops for that account and populate the Shops menu. If you need a refresher on what the interface looks like, pop back to the first chapter.

Storing Accounts

When Drizzle first initializes, if there are any accounts in `drizzleState`, we pass them to the action dispatcher `accountsFetched`, which will in turn trigger a reducer to persist them in our store. That will in turn cause our mapped `accounts` prop to change by way of `mapStateToProps`.

```
// Store the accounts when drizzle initializes
if (initialized && !prevProps.drizzleContext.initialized) {
        if (Object.keys(drizzleState.accounts).length) {
            accountsFetched(Object.values(drizzleState.accounts));
        }
}
```

Auto-selecting the First Account

When our `accounts` prop changes, and has a non-zero length, we pass its first element to the `selectAccount` action dispatcher. This will lead to our `selectedAccount` prop changing via `mapStateToProps`.

```
// Select the first account when the accounts are fetched
if (accounts && accounts.length && !prevProps.accounts) {
        selectAccount(accounts[0]);
}
```

Fetching the Selected Account's Shops

When our `selectedAccount` prop changes and is non-null, we call the `getShops` action dispatcher, passing the *StockRoom* contract (plucked by name using a constant from `drizzle.contracts`) and the `selectedAccount`.

```
// Get Shops when account is selected
if (selectedAccount &&
        selectedAccount !== prevProps.selectedAccount) {
        getShops(
            drizzle.contracts[CONTRACTS.STOCK_ROOM],
            selectedAccount
        );
}
```

Things That Can Happen On User Interaction

- Get Shops when an account is selected
- Get SKUs & SKUTypes when Shop is selected

An Account is Selected

The user will only be able to select a different account if they have connected to their local Ganache node via the Drizzle fallback configuration when MetaMask and *web3.js* are not present. Still, it can happen and falls into this category as well as the startup conditions.

```
// Get Shops when account is selected
if (selectedAccount && selectedAccount !== prevProps.selectedAc-
count) {
        getShops(
            drizzle.contracts[CONTRACTS.STOCK_ROOM],
            selectedAccount
        );
}
```

A Shop is Selected

We don't automatically select a Shop if there is one, because that we don't want to fetch too much data in case the user has multiple Shops or intends to create a new one in this session. We wait for them to make a selection or create one.

When the `selectedShop` changes and is non-null, we do the following:

- Get the Shop's balance by passing the `ProShop` contract instance, `selectedAccount`, and `selectedShopId` to the `checkShopBalance` action dispatcher
- Get the SKUTypes (categories) by passing the `StockRoom` contract instance and `selectedShopId` to the `getSKU-Types` action dispatcher
- Get the SKUs (item descriptions) by passing the `StockRoom` contract instance and `selectedShopId` to the `getSKUs` action dispatcher

```
// Get SKUs & SKUTypes when Shop is selected
if (selectedShopId &&
    selectedShopId !==
    prevProps.selectedShopId) {
        checkShopBalance(
            drizzle.contracts[CONTRACTS.PRO_SHOP],
            selectedAccount,
            selectedShopId
        );
        getSKUTypes(
            drizzle.contracts[CONTRACTS.STOCK_ROOM],
            selectedShopId
        );
        getSKUs(
            drizzle.contracts[CONTRACTS.STOCK_ROOM],
            selectedShopId
        );
}
```

Rendering the UI in the App Component

We've seen how the `App` component gets its relevant state and action dispatchers, how it automatically fetches accounts when Drizzle is initialized, automatically selects the first account, fetches the Shops when the selected account changes, and checks the Shop balance and fetches SKUs and SKUTypes when the selected Shop changes.

Now, let's see how we render the UI in the following excerpt.

```
// App.js - partial code below ...

class App extends Component {

    renderNavigation = () => {
        const {drizzle, drizzleState, initialized} =
            this.props.drizzleContext;
        return <NavigationBar
                    drizzle={drizzle}
                    drizzleState={drizzleState}
                    initialized={initialized}/>;
    };

    renderAppContent = () => {
        const {drizzle, drizzleState, initialized} =
            this.props.drizzleContext;
        return this.props.selectedShopId
            ? <ShopView
                    drizzle={drizzle}
                    drizzleState={drizzleState}
```

```
                              initialized={initialized}/>
                  : <SplashView
                              drizzle={drizzle}
                              drizzleState={drizzleState}
                              initialized={initialized}/>;
        };

        render() { return <ThemeProvider
                              theme={this.props.theme}>
            <KitWrapper>
                {this.renderNavigation()}
                {this.renderAppContent()}
            </KitWrapper>
        </ThemeProvider>;
        }

    }
```

The render function

The `render` function is sleek, and only needs to return the `NavigationBar` component and whatever is appropriate for the content section below it. It wraps these two items with the Styled Components `ThemeProvider` and our custom `KitWrapper` component, which is basically a styled HTML section element. It gets both the elements it needs to wrap from two helper functions.

```
render() { return <ThemeProvider theme={this.props.theme}>
            <KitWrapper>
                {this.renderNavigation()}
                {this.renderAppContent()}
            </KitWrapper>
        </ThemeProvider>;
}
```

The renderNavigation function

Basically, all this function does is return our custom `Naviga-tionBar` component, passing `drizzle`, `drizzleState`, and `initialized` from the DrizzleContext as props.

```
renderNavigation = () => {
    const {drizzle, drizzleState, initialized} =
        this.props.drizzleContext;
    return <NavigationBar
            drizzle={drizzle}
            drizzleState={drizzleState}
            initialized={initialized}/>;
};
```

The renderAppContent function

This function returns either a `ShopView` component or a `SplashView` component, based on whether there is a `selected-ShopId`. The returned component also has `drizzle`, `drizzle-State`, and `initialized` as props passed from the DrizzleContext.

The `SplashView` component renders the page that welcomes the user and offers a "Create Shop" form. The `ShopView` component displays and allows editing of an existing or newly created Shop.

```
renderAppContent = () => {
    const {drizzle, drizzleState, initialized} =
        this.props.drizzleContext;
    return this.props.selectedShopId
            ? <ShopView
                drizzle={drizzle}
                drizzleState={drizzleState}
                initialized={initialized}/>
            : <SplashView
                drizzle={drizzle}
```

```
                    drizzleState={drizzleState}
                    initialized={initialized}/>;
    };
```

Links

Styled Components
`bit.ly/2SxaDLB`

Summary

In this chapter, we've seen how we use Drizzle to mediate between our React client and the Ethereum API (*web3.js*).

If MetaMask is available we get the selected account from its authenticated user, otherwise, we can fallback to a websocket connection to our local Ganache instance, where we would receive multiple accounts. Accordingly, we auto-select the first account we receive and then fetch any Shops that account may have associated with it so the user can choose one to edit or create a new one if they want.

We saw how the React app manages all this and renders an appropriate screen to the user depending upon whether there is a selected Shop.

CHAPTER SEVEN

Reading Blockchain Data

Reading data from the blockchain is whole other kettle of fish from writing it. The primary difference is you don't have to pay gas for reads. You can peruse blockchain data all day long for free! Also, you can receive vast amounts of data in response to a read request, whereas there is a very strict limit to what you can write in a single transaction.

With our React application bootstrapped using Drizzle, we've arrived at a state where we have the user's Ethereum account(s) and representations of our deployed contracts available.

Immediately, we react to that state change by auto-selecting the first account and firing off a Redux action to fetch that account's existing Shops.

Next, we'll examine how actions — like the one to fetch Shops — can result in retrieval of data from the blockchain.

Shop Actions

Let's start with the action that fetches the Shops. Previously, we saw that the action dispatcher `getShops` is called from within `componentDidUpdate` of the *App* component. We skipped over what happens when that action is dispatched and focused on how the component reacts to the data when it comes in.

```
// ShopActions.js - partial code below...

import { Shop } from '../../domain';
import {
    fetchShopIds,
    fetchShops,
    createShop,
    fetchShopBalance,
    withdrawShopBalance } from '../../services/ShopService';

// Shop related actions
export const IDS_REQUESTED      = 'shop/ids-requested';
export const IDS_FETCHED        = 'shop/ids-fetched';
export const SHOPS_REQUESTED    = 'shop/items-requested';
export const SHOPS_FETCHED      = 'shop/items-fetched';

export const getShops = (contract, owner) => {

    return async function(dispatch) {

        dispatch({
            type: IDS_REQUESTED,
            fetchingIds: true,
            idsFetched: false
        });
```

```
    // Get the shop ids
    const ids = await fetchShopIds(contract, owner);

    dispatch({
        type: IDS_FETCHED,
        fetchingIds: false,
        idsFetched: true,
        ids
    });

    // Fetch the shops
    let shops;
    if (ids && ids.length) {

        dispatch({
            type: SHOPS_REQUESTED,
            fetchingShops: true,
            shopsFetched: false
        });

        shops = await fetchShops(contract, ids);
    }

    dispatch({
        type: SHOPS_FETCHED,
        fetchingShops: false,
        shopsFetched: true,
        shops
    });

    }
};
```

In the abbreviated extract of *ShopActions.js* shown here, we first import the functions which perform Shop-related interactions with our deployed contracts. Then, we define the action type constants that we're concerned with at the moment.

The "getShops" Thunk

Next, we have the `getShops` action dispatcher. It takes `contract` and `owner` arguments and operates asynchronously. For whatever nerdy reason, this type of dispatcher is called a "thunk."

Most action dispatcher functions simply return an object with a `type` property and optionally a few others. The store's `dispatch` method then passes that to the reducer where state is altered synchronously.

But when we use the *redux-thunk* library, we can return a function which takes `dispatch` as an argument and should return a `Promise`. This allows us to perform asynchronous actions like requesting data from the blockchain as well as dispatching actions.

In `getShops` we first dispatch an `IDS_REQUESTED` action, which will be processed by a reducer and update state with flags indicating that we're fetching the Shop IDs and that they haven't been fetched yet.

Then we set a constant `ids` with a call to the imported service function `fetchShopIds` using `await` to pause execution until the value is returned. We pass that function the `contract` and `owner` that we received from the UI. You may recall that the *App* component has access to `Drizzle` and thereby its contract instances. It also has all the accounts. So it has passed in the *StockRoom* contract and the selected account. From this thunk, we are passing them on to the service function which will make the actual request. While this could've been done in the component itself or in this thunk, this isolation of the contract method invocation into a separate function makes for easier unit testing.

Once the Shop IDs have been returned, we dispatch an `IDS_REQUESTED` action, with the data and the flag indicating the IDs have been fetched.

This was only the first step, though. If any IDs were returned, we now need to fetch each of the Shop Owner's Shops by ID. In that case, we dispatch a SHOPS_REQUESTED action, again allowing a reducer to update the application state with a hint as to what we're up to. When we get the Shops back, we dispatch a SHOPS_FETCHED action with the data.

Using this pattern in a thunk allows the UI to react by, for instance, showing a spinner while an async action takes place, then removing it and displaying the data when it is fetched.

Links

Redux-Thunk Repository
`bit.ly/2xsNTCL`

Shop Reducer

Now, we'll take quick peek at the reducer, which will respond to these dispatched actions by updating the application state. There's not much to discuss if you know Redux. If not, the thing to realize is that the reducer receives the current state of the store, along with the action. With those to pieces of information, it must return a new state object to replace the old one.

```
// ShopReducer - partial code below...

import {
    IDS_REQUESTED,
    IDS_FETCHED,
    SHOPS_REQUESTED,
    SHOPS_FETCHED
} from './ShopActions';

const INITIAL_STATE = {

    fetchingIds: false,
    idsFetched: false,
    ids: null,

    fetchingShops: false,
    shopsFetched: false,
    shops: [],

};

function shopReducer(state=INITIAL_STATE, action) {
    let reduced;
```

```
    switch (action.type)
    {
        case IDS_REQUESTED:
            reduced = {
                ...state,
                fetchingIds: action.fetchingIds,
                idsFetched: action.idsFetched
            };
            break;

        case IDS_FETCHED:
            reduced = {
                ...state,
                fetchingIds: action.fetchingIds,
                idsFetched: action.idsFetched,
                ids: action.ids
            };
            break;

        case SHOPS_REQUESTED:
            reduced = {
                ...state,
                fetchingShops: action.fetchingShops,
                shopsFetched: action.shopsFetched,
            };
            break;

        case SHOPS_FETCHED:
            reduced = {
                ...state,
                fetchingShops: action.fetchingShops,
                shopsFetched: action.shopsFetched,
                shops: action.shops ? action.shops : []
            };
            break;

        default:
            reduced = state;
    }
    return reduced;
}

export default shopReducer;
```

Once the reducer has returned the updated state, the components that map that state to props will render again. In this case, updating the Shops menu with the Shops that were returned, if any.

Links

Redux Website
`redux.js.org/introduction/getting-started`

Shop Service

This little ES6 module is were we actually invoke the Shop-related contract methods, getting data back from the blockchain. Here's an extract from *ShopService.js* that shows how we get the Shop IDs and Shops:

```js
// ShopService.js - partial code below...

import { Shop } from '../domain';

/**
 * Fetch the Shop Ids for the given owner account
 * @param contract
 * @param owner
 * @returns {number[]}
 */
export const fetchShopIds = async (contract, owner) => {

    return await contract.methods.getShopIds(owner).call();
};

/**
 * Fetch the Shops for the given list of Shop Ids
 * @param contract
 * @param ids
 * @returns {Shop[]}
 */
export const fetchShops = async (contract, ids) => {

    let promises = ids.map(id =>
contract.methods.getShop(id).call());
```

```
    let shopArrays = await Promise.all(promises);

    return shopArrays.map( shopArray =>
Shop.fromArray(shopArray) );

};
```

First, we import something called `Shop` from the `domain` folder. *Shop.js* defines a class that represents the `Shop` domain entity. It is a JavaScript mirror of our Solidity struct that has methods for validating the entire object and its individual fields, as well as factory methods for creating a new `Shop` instance from an ordinary JavaScript object or from an array of values, which is how a `Shop` is returned in pieces from the `getShop` contract method.

As we saw in the `getShops` thunk, getting the user's Shops is a two step process. We get the IDs of all the Shops in one call, then we make another call that fetches each corresponding Shop.

The "fetchShopIds" Function

Here, in our `fetchShopIds` function (so named to avoid confusion with the action dispatcher `getShops` that calls it), we make an async call to `contract.methods.getShopIds`, passing the owner address, and invoking `call` on the returned function.

```
export const fetchShopIds = async (contract, owner) => {

    return await contract.methods.getShopIds(owner).call();
};
```

You may have noticed that this is a little different from the syntax we used in our contract unit tests, which arose from Truffle framework's contract abstraction. The `contract` object that Drizzle has provided us is a *web3.js* contract instance instead.

Still, this is pretty straightforward stuff. We're just going to return the array of Shop IDs (which may be empty) that we get back from this call. The thunk will then examine the results and call our `fetchShops` function if any IDs were returned.

The "fetchShops" Function

In the `fetchShops` function, we map the array of IDs to an array of promises, each of which is returned from an invocation of `call` on `contract.methods.getShop` where we pass in the ID at the array index being mapped.

```
export const fetchShops = async (contract, ids) => {

    let promises = ids.map(id =>
contract.methods.getShop(id).call());

    let shopArrays = await Promise.all(promises);

    return shopArrays.map( shopArray =>
Shop.fromArray(shopArray) );

};
```

Then we await the resolution of all the promises, which will be deposited into a constant `shopArrays`. Recall that the contract's `getShop` method returns an array containing the properties of the indicated Shop struct.

We now have an array of arrays representing all the user's Shops. We need to turn that into an array of Shop instances. That's easily done by mapping the `shopArrays` array and invoking `Shop.fromArray` on each element. The result is returned immediately, where the thunk will pass it to the reducer in a SHOP-

S_FETCHED action, the application state will be updated, triggering update of the UI, specifically the Shops menu on the *NavigationBar* component.

Links

Web3 Contracts
`bit.ly/2M1UOeF`

Summary

We've seen in this chapter how a "thunk" (or asynchronous action dispatcher) can be invoked from the UI, call a service function that reads blockchain data via a contract function call, which returns asynchronously, passing the result to a reducer to update application state.

Service functions are separated from the UI and action dispatcher code so that they can be mocked for unit testing.

CHAPTER EIGHT

Writing Blockchain Data

Now, we'll examine the more complicated scenario of writing data to the blockchain, which requires the following steps:

- Our application to send a transaction to the contract
- An event to be dispatched by the contract after writing the data
- Our application to listen for and respond to the event

We've just seen how to fetch the user's existing Shops. Now, let's see how we can actually create one.

Fetching data from a contract is basically the same as any async query you might make to an ordinary database-backed API. That's because it doesn't entail creation of blockchain transactions or events.

The process of writing data will be a tad more complicated.

When you invoke a function that writes data, you actually send a transaction rather than make a call, and you receive a promise that resolves to the 32-bit transaction hash, not the return value of the function.

That transaction hash is a handle to the finished transaction that was written on the blockchain, which contains the loads of details, including the block number, gas used, etc.

But that's generally not what you want in the client after firing off this transaction. In this particular case, what we want is the Shop ID that was assigned to our new Shop.

How do we get the data we're actually after? We listen for the event that was emitted from the function we sent the transaction to. To understand how this works, let's return to our *ShopService* module and its `createShop` function.

Shop Service

```
// ShopService.js - partial code below...

import { Shop } from '../domain';
import { EVENTS } from '../constants';

/**
 * Create a new Shop
 * @param contract
 * @param name
 * @param description
 * @param fiat
 * @param owner
 */
export const createShop = async (
    contract,
    owner,
    name,
    description,
    fiat,
    callback) => {

    contract
      .events[EVENTS.NEW_SHOP]({owner: owner})
      .once('data', callback);

    contract
      .methods
      .createShop(name, description, fiat)
      .send({from: owner});

};
```

The "createShop" Function

As you might expect, the function takes all the properties of a new Shop. They were collected from the Create Shop form and passed to a another thunk called fetchShops in *ShopActions.js*.

But there's one more argument to the createShop function: callback. And notice that this function (createShop) doesn't return anything. Consequently, you might expect the fetchShops thunk in *ShopActions.js* will have a different implementation from the getShops one we saw before. We'll follow up on that in a moment.

The first thing this function does is set a one-time listener for the NewShop event that's emitted from the createShop function on the deployed *StockRoom* contract. It does that by using our EVENTS.NEW_SHOP constant to select the appropriate event handle in the *web3.js* contract instance. It filters the events coming from that contract to those where the owner property is equal to our owner address. Finally, it invokes once on the returned object specifying that the very next event of this type should be passed to the callback function, and then the listener should be removed.

With the event listener set up, it proceeds to send the transaction by passing the rest of the arguments to contract.methods.createShop, and invoking send instead of call on the returned object. In our send invocation, we pass a config argument with the from property set to our owner address.

When the Shop is created in the deployed contract and the transaction written to the blockchain, an event will be emitted. We'll receive that event in the callback function that was passed in as the last argument to this createShop service function.

Now, let's pop back over to *ShopActions.js* and have a look at the thunk that invoked createShop.

Shop Actions

```
// Service functions
import { createShop} from '../../services/ShopService';
import { Shop } from '../../domain';


// Shop related actions
export const SHOP_SELECTED      = 'shop/selected';
export const CREATING_SHOP      = 'shop/creating';
export const SHOP_CREATED       = 'shop/created';

export const selectShop = shopId => {

    return {
        type: SHOP_SELECTED,
        selectedShopId: shopId
    };

};

export const createNewShop = (
    contract, owner, name, description, fiat) => {

    return async function(dispatch) {

        dispatch({
            type: CREATING_SHOP,
            creatingShop: true,
            owner,
            name,
            description,
            fiat
        });
```

```
createShop(
    contract,
    owner,
    name,
    description,
    fiat,
    event => {

        const shopId = event.returnValues[1];

        const shop = new Shop(
          owner, shopId, name, description, fiat
        );

        dispatch({
          type: SHOP_CREATED,
          shop,
          creatingShop: false
        });

        dispatch(selectShop(shop.shopId));
    } );

  };

};
```

The "createNewShop" Thunk

This thunk doesn't look that much different than the one we used to fetch the Shop IDs and Shops before.

Similarly, it's invoked from a component in the UI and is passed the all the arguments we'll need to get the job done, including the contract instance and selected account (from Drizzle) as well as the fields required to create a new Shop.

Also, following the previous thunk's pattern, we immediately dispatch a CREATING_SHOP action, so that the UI can react by hiding the form's submit button and replacing it with an spinner.

Then it calls the imported `createShop` service function. And this is where it deviates from the previous thunk's implementation.

Rather than awaiting a return value and then dispatching another action, it instead passes an anonymous function as the last argument of the call. That anonymous function takes an argument called `event`.

Remember how the `createShop` service function's event listener invokes the `callback` function that we pass it? Well, this is that callback. This is where we take the data in that event and add it to our application state.

What will the event look like?

```
/**
 * @dev emitted upon creation of a shop
 * @return uint256 shopId
 */
event NewShop(
  address indexed owner,
  uint256 shopId,
  string name);
```

In our *ShopFactory.sol* contract, we declare the new `NewShop` event that gets emitted when `createShop` has added the new Shop to the contract's state. Since the first argument — `owner` — is indexed, we were able to filter this event by owner in our `create-Shop` service function. The second argument is `shopId`, and that's what we're interested in now.

In our anonymous callback function, we get the `shopId` from the `event.returnValues` array at index 1. Then, we create a new `Shop` entity from the data we already have plus the `shopId`, and dispatch a `SHOP_CREATED` action. That action passes the new `Shop` to the reducer where it will be added to the owner's Shops in our store.

Finally, we'll dispatch one more action; `SHOP_SELECTED`, using the simple action dispatcher `shopSelected`. This is the same action dispatcher that would be used if the user clicked on a Shop in the Shops menu.

Shop Reducer

Next, it's worth having a quick look at how the reducer deals with the `CREATING_SHOP`, `SHOP_CREATED`, and `SHOP_SELECTED` actions.

```
import {
    SHOP_SELECTED,
    CREATING_SHOP,
    SHOP_CREATED,
} from './ShopActions';

const INITIAL_STATE = {
    newShop: {
        owner: null,
        name: "",
        description: "",
        fiat: "USD"
    },
    creatingShop: false,
    selectedShopId: null,
    fetchingShopBalance: false,
    shopBalanceFetched: false,
    selectedShopBalance: 0

};

function shopReducer(state=INITIAL_STATE, action) {
    let reduced;
    switch (action.type)
    {

        case SHOP_SELECTED:
```

```
            reduced = {
                ...state,
                selectedShopId:
                  action.selectedShopId,
                fetchingShopBalance:
                  INITIAL_STATE.fetchingShopBalance,
                shopBalanceFetched:
                  INITIAL_STATE.shopBalanceFetched,
                selectedShopBalance:
                  INITIAL_STATE.selectedShopBalance,
                withdrawingBalance:
                  INITIAL_STATE.withdrawingBalance,
                balanceWithdrawn:
                  INITIAL_STATE.balanceWithdrawn

            };
            break;

        case CREATING_SHOP:
            reduced = {
                ...state,
                creatingShop: action.creatingShop,
                newShop: {
                    owner: action.owner,
                    name: action.name,
                    description: action.description,
                    fiat: action.fiat
                }
            };
            break;

        case SHOP_CREATED:
            reduced = {
                ...state,
                ids: state.ids.concat([action.shop.shopId]),
                shops: state.shops.concat([action.shop]),
                creatingShop: action.creatingShop,
                newShop: INITIAL_STATE.newShop
            };
            break;

        default:
            reduced = state;
    }
    return reduced;
```

```
}

export default shopReducer;
```

Note that the `SHOP_SELECTED` case basically just sets the selected Shop's ID and resets all the other state elements related to the selected shop to their values as represented in `INITIAL_STATE`.

In the case of `CREATING_SHOP`, we place all the form values that were sent to the action dispatcher into the `newShop` section of Shop-related state and set the `creatingShop` flag.

Finally, to handle `SHOP_CREATED`, we replace the array of Shop IDs with a copy that has the new Shop's ID added to the end. Likewise, we replace the array of Shops with a copy that has the new Shop entity added. We clear the `creatingShop` flag and reset the `newShop` object to its representation in `INITIAL_STATE`.

Create New Shop UI

Since we're assuming you understand or are at least passingly familiar with React and Redux, a full description of the UI components used to display the form and call the action dispatcher on submission is academic. I only touch on it here for a sense of closure for this use case.

There are validated fields for Shop Name and Description, a radio button selector for fiat currency, and a submit button labeled "Create" that gets replaced by a spinner while `creatingShop` is true in the application state. The fields are filled by the `newShop` section of state that we saw in *ShopReducer.js*.

The mechanics of the form are uninteresting, and to include the source code here would raise more questions than it answers because of the use of the Styled Components and Bootstrap libraries as well as the custom component kit created for this app.

If you're interested, have a look in the project source at *Splash-View.js* which instantiates *ShopForm.js* shown here. To explore how the components are themed, root around in the *src/components/ theme* folder, and the custom component kit in *src/components/theme/ kit*.

Summary

Calling a contract method that merely returns data can be done with async/await or ordinary promise handling. However, when sending a transaction that will write data to the contract, we will need to listen for the event emitted by the method we sent the transaction to.

When listening for events, we can filter by any indexed properties of the event, such as the owner of the Shop, so that we don't inadvertently respond to events generated by other users.

In this chapter, we saw how all this fits within the framework of a React application using Redux to maintain state.

CHAPTER NINE

Deployment

Up until now, we've used a Ganache-CLI Ethereum installation for local deployment and testing of our contracts. For all intents and purposes, it *is* the blockchain to us. No one else can see our code or our transactions. And while Ganache gives our accounts 100 ETH by default, we can give ourselves as much as we like using the `—defaultBalanceEther` option, so we can test to our hearts' content in our safe little cocoon.

But at some point, we have put it out there on a testnet. Mainly, to make absolutely certain it works. And to let other developers start interacting with our contracts. In this chapter, we'll find out what's involved in making that leap.

Frontend Deployment

According to BlockchainHub, the frontend of a dApp *can* be deployed to a decentralized network such as Swarm or IPFS. Like Ethereum itself, these networks use decentralization to ensure that no one computer (and thus no one person or organization) has control of the data or application.

That's a wonderful concept, but there are a few problems with it at the moment:

- The networks are just too slow.
- The gateways are too few and often offline.
- They serve only static files, which precludes optimizations like server-side rendering of a React or Angular app.

In the future, perhaps this situation will change, but I doubt it. The main thing that we want decentralized and immutable is the data such as ownership of tokens, or records of transactions. And that resides in our contracts, deployed to the blockchain.

Build the React App

Thus far we've been running the local server the Create React App scripts offer us while developing. Now we need a production build. Internally, the Create React App script for creating the production build will use Webpack to compress everything for an optimized download experience.

After completing the following steps, you should end up with a *build* folder containing the deployable files. Only that folder needs to be deployed.

1. In *package.json*, change the `homepage` entry to be the URL you'll be deploying to. This is important because React infers certain things about the location of assets based on this entry.

2. Build the React application with following command: `npm run app:build`

Pick a Hosting Service

For this project, deployment only requires an ordinary hosting service. If you have a hosting provider you're happy with, just skip the following parts. For instance, you could use Github Pages if you wanted. In this case, we've already set up Github Pages for the project to serve a docs page, so we'll need to host the app elsewhere.

For our purposes, we'll use Firebase. Google offers a most generous free tier with their Firebase hosting product. And it's possible that we will want to extend the application with a backend that tracks usage or provides other off-chain services. Firebase's real-time NoSQL database, cloud functions, and cloud messaging make it an excellent platform choice for the growth potential it offers.

In order to achieve this, only a few steps are necessary. I won't go into great detail since it's an aside from the business of writing an Ethereum dApp, much as using Styled Components for applying CSS to the UI components was not integral to understanding the process, but was an ancillary decision for making the app look pretty.

If you know Firebase, this will be old hat. If not, you might have to read a few paragraphs of their docs along the way while the following these basic steps. It'll be worth it, though. Firebase is awesome. But again, any hosting service will do, and the app itself isn't dependent upon Firebase in any way.

Deploying to Firebase

We're not talking to the Firebase backend from our client, only hosting it, so it's quite easy to deploy the project:

1. Go to the Firebase website and create an account or log into your console if you already have an account.
2. Create a new project.
3. Connect a custom domain or subdomain to your project on the hosting tab OR take note of the project url (e.g., `https://myproj.firebaseapp.com`).
4. Install the Firebase tools on your development machine if you don't already have them: `npm install -g firebase-tools`
5. Log in with the account used to create the project: `firebase login`

6. Create a *.firebaserc* file with the name of the project set as default. The one in the project points to the project name I've deployed it to. If you're deploying a copy of the project for testing, you'll need to change this to the project name that you just created in step 2.

7. Create a *firebase.json* file, which will tell the firebase tools what directory to deploy, what files to ignore when uploading, and what headers to send when someone requests the site. The one in the project should work perfectly without modification.

8. Deploy the application to hosting: `firebase deploy`

Links

BlockchainHub on dApp deployment
`bit.ly/2GJZPVY`

What is Swarm and What is it Used For?
`bit.ly/2KlxupP`

IPFS Website
`ipfs.io`

IPFS Public Gateway Status
`bit.ly/2YihRsW`

How Create React App Uses homepage in *package.json*
`bit.ly/33cqAvx`

GitHub Pages
`pages.github.com`

Firebase Hosting
`firebase.google.com`

Contract Deployment

As you're aware by now, deploying contracts and testing them costs Ether. We have plenty of that available to us on our local Ganache-CLI instance, albeit simulated and only usable locally. But on the Ethereum **mainnet**, we need *actual* cryptocurrency to deploy.

Fortunately, before we have to make that plunge, there are the **testnets**. And with them, faucets.

Pick a Testnet

There are a number of public testnets out there. The most popular, perhaps due to support from Etherscan and Infura are:

- **Ropsten** – Cross client testnet
- **Rinkeby** – Geth client testnet
- **Kovan** – Parity client testnet
- **Görli** – POA client testnet

We'll deploy to Ropsten, because it's the oldest and most well known. But how do we do that?

You can deploy via Remix, the Ethereum browser-based IDE. However, with a project of this scale, you don't want to be cutting and pasting the contracts into the browser. That's mainly for simple experiments.

We could also deploy with a fully functional network node, which is a bit beyond the scope of what we're trying to do. That's generally what you want to have in order to set up an mining operation.

For a non-trivial project such as ours, Infura is our easiest way to deploy to a testnet. Infura is free to use. It was created within Consensys which also brings us, among other amazing projects, the Truffle Framework and MetaMask, which we're already quite cozy with.

First, however, we need some faux Ether so we can deploy to Ropsten via Infura.

Get Some Ether from a Faucet

You presumably have MetaMask installed by now, but if not, head on over to their website and install the plugin it in your Chrome or Firefox browser. If you're just installing it, while you are there, be sure to watch the video that's embedded in their page. It describes how to operate MetaMask and is very helpful if you're not familiar with it.

Next, make sure the **Ropsten Test Network** is selected as shown in the screenshot.

Now go to the MetaMask Ether Faucet and request some Ether by clicking the big green button. You will be asked to allow the faucet to connect to your Account.

You'll see the transaction id and if you click it, it will take you to Etherscan, where you'll see that the transaction is pending.

In a minute or so the transaction will clear and you should be good to go. You now have enough play Ether on Ropsten to deploy your contracts.

MetaMask Ether Faucet

faucet

address: 0x81b7e08f65bdf5648606c89998a9cc8164397647
balance: ...

request 1 ether from faucet

Copy your Seed Phrase

MetaMask created an account for your use, into which you just added 1 Ether. But in order for us to deploy using that account, we need the "seed phrase" or "mnemonic". It is a set of words that are used to generate your public and private keys.

1.   Click the Account Avatar on the right side of the MetaMask popup.
2.   Click the Settings menu option.
3.   Click the Security and Privacy menu option.
4.   Click the Reveal Seed Words button.
5.   Enter your password to reveal the Seed Words then click the Copy To Clipboard button.

Deploy with Infura

This is a super streamlined process so, hold on to your hat!

1. Go to the Infura website and create an account or log into your dashboard if you already have an account.
2. Click the "Create Project" button on the dashboard and give your project a name.
3. You'll see all the keys and urls associated with the project now. Copy the Project ID.
4. Edit the *truffle.js* file and update the URL for Ropsten network with your Project ID and your MetaMask Seed Phrase (which you copied to the clipboard earlier).
5. Migrate contracts with the command: `truffle deploy — network ropsten`

Links

Partial List of Known Network IDs
`bit.ly/2LYJ6SN`

Etherscan Website
`etherscan.io`

Infura Website
`infura.io`

Deploying to Ropsten from Remix
`bit.ly/2Kf6FEP`

MetaMask Ether Faucet
`faucet.metamask.io`

Testing the Deployment

Now the contracts and application are deployed, and they should be able talk to each other. The moment of truth has arrived!

Generate Transactions in the App

Navigate to the web URL where you deployed the app and it should ask if you want to allow the app to connect to your account via MetaMask. Click Accept and you should be able to create Shops, Categories, and Items.

If you're just following along, and haven't actually deployed anything, you can still give it a whirl, just head on over to `https://iaps-test.futurescale.com`.

That's an instance of this project deployed as described above. If the app doesn't appear to connect or you don't see the MetaMask popup asking you for permission to connect to your account, kill your browser and launch it again.

After filling out the New Shop form, for instance, MetaMask will show you the terms of the transaction and ask if you want to confirm it.

In this case, there is no actual Ether amount to be transferred, only the gas fee.

View Transactions on Etherscan

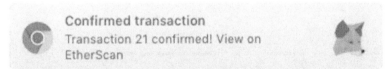

After what seems like forever (maybe half a minute), MetaMask will notify you that the transaction is complete. If you click the browser notification, it will take you to Etherscan where you can view the details of the completed transaction.

In the app, when you are connected to a network supported by Etherscan, you can view the account on Etherscan from the Accounts menu.

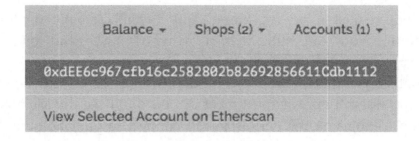

However you get there, Etherscan's page for an address shows all the transactions for that address as well as its balance. The From and To addresses are links. They take you to the the account that initiated the transaction and the contract that received it.

Summary

While deployment of your application will depend on your preferred hosting platform, the contracts are a different matter. There are a number of testnets available, and deployment to them can be achieved easily using a free Infura account. Using MetaMask, you can create an account on these networks, and fund them with faux ether using "faucets". Getting your dApp working on a testnet is critical, as sadly, the mainnet has no faucet; you'll be spending cold hard ether for every transaction.

CHAPTER TEN

Next Steps

We've surveyed the Ethereum development landscape, made some hard decisions about the tech stack, built a local environment, written contracts, tested them, bootstrapped a client, made it read and write blockchain data, and finally deployed it to a testnet.

Now what?

Hop on the Train

The Ethereum ecosystem is a fast-moving train; if you want to ride, you just have to run alongside and hop into an open boxcar. Reading alone cannot give you the skills you'll need. Until you find something to spend a little time on and begin solving your own problems, you'll always be jogging alongside the train.

At this point, hopefully, you have:

- Checked out the In-App-Pro-Shop project from GitHub
- The tests passing
- The contracts migrated
- The mock data added
- The React application communicating with MetaMask and maintaining a Shop

This means you have some contracts to talk to and a local Ganache instance you can communicate with from a different application.

A possible next step might be to build an interface for making in-app purchases, such as you'd include in a game. You could create a separate project, build an app (using React, or any other front-end tech you may fond of) and connect to the *StockRoom* contract, retrieve your Shop, SKUTypes, SKUs and present an interface that lets a user find items to purchase. Then use the `ProShop` contract to allow them to make purchases.

Since both the React app and the contracts are already familiar and handy for reference, you might find this little exercise easier than starting an entirely new dApp. If you complete such an exercise, please feel free to open an issue on the In-App ProShop project on GitHub, with a link to your repo.

Of course if you've made it this far, you've probably come up with plenty of ideas of your own along the way. You might just want to jump right into building one of those.

Whatever you do, I encourage you to start building something without delay, while all this is fresh in your mind. Else, you may find that what you've learned here quickly fades and when you finally do get around to building something in, say, six months, the whole landscape will have changed.

Stay Current

The Solidity documentation site has this to say on the matter:

> When deploying contracts, you should use the latest released version of Solidity. This is because breaking changes as well as new features and bug fixes are introduced regularly. We currently use a 0.x version number to indicate this fast pace of change.

When I began working on In-App ProShop, the Solidity version was 0.4.24. The code in this book has been revised several times since then. It now stands at 0.5.12. Meanwhile, the most recent version as of this writing is 0.6.0.

I would have updated the code to the latest version, except the OpenZeppelin contracts that it extends have not been updated themselves, and so the compiler throws an error. Be prepared for this sort of frustration. As Ethereum changes, all the dependencies you use to work with it need to change as well. Don't hesitate to gently prod the owners of those projects you depend upon to get a move on so you can get your own code upgraded.

The In-App ProShop project repository will be updated, and inevitably move out of sync with the code in this book. As time goes by, be sure to study the repo code rather than relying on this book's code as a reference. It is only included here as a convenience to provide context. As such, it is just a blurry snapshot of a fast-moving train.

Another warning on the Solidity documentation site is this:

> Solidity recently released the 0.6.x version that introduced a lot of breaking changes. Make sure you read the full list.

Each time Solidity is upgraded, there are usually breaking changes. Hopefully after `1.0.0`, this will settle down, but it's still early days. Things move fast and get broken all the time. Keeping up with it all is the price one pays for living on the so-called "bleeding edge." The upside is that you have the opportunity to shape this new technology. Push boundaries. Create something entirely new.

Wave Goodbye

With those parting suggestions, this book comes to a close.

I hope you've enjoyed this introduction to Solidity development and will get some use out of the project — whether you're just learning Ethereum, or looking to build on it to enable in-app purchases.

Good luck on your journey.

Links

Solidity Docs
`bit.ly/2XkrtTw`

In-App Pro Shop
`bit.ly/2KXnohH`

Contact the Author
`cliffordhall.com/interrupt-me`

Enjoy this book?

Please consider writing a review on Amazon or Goodreads!